CORSETS TO CAMOUFLAGE

Phyllis

a favourite book gift for
a lady who made awful
sandwiches and talked too much
and whose company surprisingly
I enjoyed in May 2006
for a fortnight while on a
daring visit to Scotland

Alex
xxx

Author's Acknowledgements

Professor Charles Thomas for all his help with research, and Nigel Steel and Terry Charman of the Imperial War Museum for their historical expertise; and Christopher Dowling who invited me to write in conjunction with the Museum's exhibition. A great number of people have been immensely kind with their time and advice, especially the staff at Sunderland City Library's local studies department, and Lindsay Fulcher, Assistant Editor of *The Lady*.

On military matters, there have been numerous comments and help, in particular from Sir Jeremy MacKenzie and Sir Rupert Smith. I'm grateful to my editor Rowena Webb and to Juliet Brightmore at Hodder & Stoughton, also to Esther Jagger, Kerry Hood and Jacqui Lewis. Louise Greenberg, for her unfailing encouragement. All those women who allowed me to record their memories, especially those in the Ack Ack, the Land Army and the Aycliffe Angels.

Note on British money in pre-decimal days
12d (pence) = 1s (shilling)
20s = £1

CORSETS TO CAMOUFLAGE

Women and War

Kate Adie

coronet

CORONET BOOKS

Hodder & Stoughton

Text copyright © 2003 by Kate Adie

For illustrations and photographs copyrights
see Photo Acknowledgements, page 294

First published in Great Britain in 2003 by Hodder and Stoughton
A division of Hodder Headline

This paperback edition published in 2004

A Coronet paperback

1 3 5 7 9 10 8 6 4 2

A CIP catalogue record for this title is available from the British Library

ISBN 0 340 82060 8

Typeset in Sabon by Palimpsest Book Production Limited,
Polmont, Stirlingshire

Printed and bound Mackays of Chatham Ltd, Chatham, Kent

Hodder and Stoughton
A division of Hodder Headline
338 Euston Road
London NW1 3BH

CONTENTS

INTRODUCTION

N OUTLINE, IN silhouette, just a glimpse – a soldier's boots, perhaps a policeman's helmet, or a glint of gold braid – all have powerful impact. And my first encounter with women in uniform is fixed in my memory as two pairs of dreadful legs, descending – nay bulging – into two clomping pairs of shoes.

In the mid-fifties it was the custom in my nice girls' school in Sunderland to expose us to the wider world through the occasional Wednesday Talk. However, instead of lectures from the Great and the Good, our militant Anglican foundation, Sunderland Church High School, produced a steady stream of the Pious or Slightly Deranged. We'd spot them heading up the main staircase, a vivid splash of long purple skirt swishing around big black boots. 'Another batty bishop from Bongoland,' we'd hiss, before composing our features for a peroration on the mischief wrought by termites upon prayer books, or the difficulties of steering the diocesan dug-out canoe through mangrove swamps.

The occasional highbrow musician was also deemed acceptable, with the memorable Florence Hooton wielding her cello like a table-tennis bat, and then announcing to a stupefied gaggle of adolescent females that she was 'about to put a very powerful instrument between my legs'. Then, one Wednesday, the staircase resounded to a particularly firm tread. Stomp stomp stomp. The headmistress's thick ankles and sensible court shoes looked positively skittish, flanked as they were by an escort of biliously coloured tree trunks.

We lifted our gaze slowly upwards. The skirts hung like cardboard, just at the length which makes your calves look fat and suggests your thighs are like a couple of marrows. Further up were jackets of unforgiving cut, boxy and mannish, restraining what were undoubtedly formidable bosoms. The bosoms swayed a fraction out of sync with the swinging arms and the marching gait. Starched collars and ties concealed what necks there might have been, as the pair pincered the headmistress between the assembly hall doors. Their expressions were impossible to read, for it appeared they wore shiny caps perched on their noses. How they saw was a mystery. They turned smartly to ascend the platform, two rhino rears in rhythmic harmony.

I cannot recall a single word of the lecture addressed to us. The entire impact was visual. Here were two grown-ups, people who'd achieved the enviable womanhood we yearned for, apparently dressed – well, not so much dressed as upholstered – in a manner which defied analysis. Yes, they were uniforms – but not of the familiar sagging bus conductress variety. These were bandbox-sharp with glinty buttons, spotless, with ironed-flat pockets where no balled-up old hankie would dare to lurk. We girls were being introduced to the Women's Royal Army Corps and the Women's Royal Air Force. One dark green, one blue, sort-of.

It was the legs which really fascinated. Our girlish dreams were of spiky heels and pointy toes in ice-cream colours (or perhaps scarlet if you dared to be 'fast'). Of the palest nylons with sexy black seams – perhaps the tiniest butterfly bow peeping from just above the heel. This was what lay in store after years of school uniform, with our dreams contained by regulation Indoor and Outdoor Shoes, both modelled on fishboxes, and a choice of wrinkly grey socks or hairy knee-stockings. And here were two women who'd seemingly chosen to encase their legs in some kind of ancient lisle, vaguely reminiscent of something seen in the dusty windows of surgical appliance suppliers. And who had acquired footwear suitable for marching on Moscow.

Our teenage imaginations trembled. And there and then, I decided that uniforms were not for me.

Nor did I come from a military family. World War II was over when I was born, and the easy familiarity with khaki and blue had disappeared instantly in peacetime. Admittedly, my home town in north-east England was a fruitful recruiting ground for the Durham Light Infantry, and the occasional warship was heaved into the mouth of the River Wear by over-enthusiastic tugs, pranging the inner piers. But we had no barracks or local air station, only strange fields where concrete squares marked the floors of a wartime army camp, and unpleasantly ponging concrete 'pillboxes' lurking below the coastal cliffs, still ready to defend our shores.

Except for the plentiful bomb-sites on which we children played, Sunderland having been pasted regularly by the Germans, I assumed that this ship-building town and its people had been only peripherally involved in the two world wars. The men had 'gone off to have a crack at Jerry'; the women had stayed to 'keep the home fires burning.' I had little inkling of the extent to which an ordinary industrial town had found itself inexorably drawn into war, a place where daily life changed fundamentally twice in the twentieth century, as far distant events affected life, work, and the north-east skies overhead. I never guessed at the extraordinary extent to which everyone had been 'in the wars' – especially the women. Maids who became munitions workers, schoolgirls on fire-watch, housewives who joined voluntary units, and all those who joined the services. Military history is a male preserve, dominated by the image of the male warrior. Nevertheless, the unprecedented progress of women towards equality during the twentieth century is brought into sharp relief by war, although that progress often went unnoticed, and unsung, behind the striking deeds of valour on the battlefield.

I'm reminded of an exchange between my first Newcastle landlady and her neighbour, when I was a student in the sixties:

'Your husband was away four years, wasn't he?'

'Aye, he was, North Africa with Monty, and he never stopped about the sand and the flies . . .'

'What can you say. . . .'

'Well, I could've said about the air-raid sirens, the black-out, the bombs, the rationing . . . but I didn't.'

'Ever talk about your job in the RAF?'

'He wasn't interested in welding.'

I regarded my landlady with curiosity: a very short, wiry Geordie widow, who was always asking me to sort out 'men's work' around the house – wonky electric plugs, the ancient Hoover and so on.

Welding?

So, years ago, in the aftermath of World War II, I'd had intimations of a different life for women in wartime, but no sense of its significance, and certainly no interest in uniforms and all that they conveyed.

And as a child, there was already a certain amount of prejudice residing in my soul. I'd been a Brownie, and had discovered that In The Pack no element of individuality was entertained. All Brownies wore turd-coloured bag-like shifts, with a leather belt and a custard yellow tie. Fatter Brownies looked like hamsters feeding permanently on a banana. The outfit was surmounted by a chocolate-coloured knitted Thing, which slid off your head the moment you had to do some Brownie ritual, usually involving imaginary toadstools. If you were diligent your sleeve was peppered with weird symbols, proclaiming your status as a girl well versed in raffia-craft or whatever. The good aspect of the uniform was that it blended into the dust and dirt which was swirled up by Brownie Games in dingy church halls and left over wartime prefab huts. In other words, it worked, but did nothing for you. Still, in the days before preteen fashion-aware culture took hold, none of us minded much.

For a start, everyone wore school uniform, which was clearly designed by someone who disliked children, especially girls. Decades on, the subject of the Horrible School Hat still provokes wrath and despair among my contemporaries. Ditto the School Divided Skirt ('no girl shall wear a skirt which is more than two inches from the floor when kneeling'). Then there was the School Winter Coat, a creation which had a life of its own. So hairy and stiff that, when new, it stood by itself without visible support. You didn't exactly wear it, you engaged with it, and once you were lined up in the daily crocodile, two by two, you were described by onlookers as The Russian Army off to the Front. But there was always joy to be derived from the fact that other schools clearly employed professional tailoring sadists to produce even more ludicrous and demeaning styles. And then there was the one good aspect: absolutely no decisions to be made in the morning. No agonising in and out of the wardrobe. Just climb into the same old stuff and all will be right with the world.

So at a very early age, I'd sampled the impact of uniforms: their power to deliver an instantaneous message, their ability to reduce the individual to a unit, simultaneously marking you out and blending you in.

As my teens approached, the Girl Guides made overtures. Whatever the excitements of more badges and a bit of damp camping, I was becoming aware that evenings spent in a blue bag-like sack, plus beret, were not exactly seductive-sounding. And so it was that the arrival of the WRAC and WRAF, stomp stomp stomp, sealed my views on uniforms and aroused my curiosity.

CHAPTER ONE

MAIDS IN ARMOUR

EVEN IN MY obscure world of Scandinavian Studies at university, war and battles intruded. Monday mornings were spent in seminars trying to figure out just how many ways a Viking could vanquish his enemy, all involving an axe, a tree and an unfortunate amount of exposed intestine. Down through history came the names of warriors, carved elegantly in runic letters on to huge standing stones. Language commemorated frenzied fighting by those wearing bear-shirts – going berserk. Songs celebrated heroic deeds, centuries after they happened. Men of valour bestrode history – but only a few women could be glimpsed through the fog of war.

Student parties in the 1960s were crowded, unglamorous affairs in Newcastle. Nevertheless one night I headed for the bathroom of a particularly grubby flat in the student-infested suburb of Jesmond only to find Queen Elizabeth I perched on the edge of the bath, a bottle of Newcastle Brown Ale in her hand.

Dame Flora Robson *was* the Virgin Queen, everyone's Tudor icon, etched into cinema history in *Fire Over England*, one of those sweeping historical romps which gripped audiences in the grey days of war. A vision of velvet and pearls, starched ruff above a polished steel breastplate as she addressed her troops at Tilbury, ready to take on the dastardly Spanish. The white horse pawed the ground, the soldiers' armour glittered, the pennants on the lances fluttered and the words rang out: 'I know I have the body of a weak and feeble woman, but I have the heart and stomach of a king, and a king of England too; and think foul scorn that Parma or Spain, or any prince of Europe, should dare to invade the borders of my realm.' Cue much cheering from the front stalls.

The vision in the bathroom was wearing a dowdy brown dress rather than slashed brocade and silk. Dame Flora was a warm, down-to-earth woman, born in South Shields, who happened to be visiting the small theatre in Jesmond that bore her name, and she'd unexpectedly answered the university Dramatic Society's party invitation. A practical, observant actress, she regaled us with stories of the behind-the-scenes lunacies of film-making, especially the dratted horse at Tilbury which had had a mind of its own and very active bowels. Wearing a breastplate over a dress boned and stuffed like a Christmas turkey had been no picnic either, and the horse had been in total agreement, going into a huge sulk at the umpteenth take and sagging un-regally, ears back.

On screen, though, it was romantic perfection, evoking the ultimate warrior-queen, an inspiration at the head of her troops; a figure that has ridden through history in and out of the mist of battle, giving rise to legend and not a little sexual *frisson*. Boadicea and Joan of Arc, Japanese empresses and Celtic queens, assorted Germanic women and Roman gladiatrixes, Saxon leaders and, of course, Amazons: there is a long and rather fuzzy list of names which confirms the potency of the image, but is rather short on detail. The list grows longer as a feminist view of history digs for concealed heroines, the victims of male prejudice, air-brushed out of official history. However, the subservient position which has been the lot of women in most societies for centuries underlines the significance of attitudes held by all, not just men. Where women lacked legal status, had no political power, were deemed lesser creatures by the official religion, and belonged to the huge majority tied to hearth and home through children and lack of money, the creature who broke out and flourished a sword in the ultimate masculine world of war was truly exceptional; even, the twentieth century, with well-documented world wars, gives ample evidence of the automatic relegation of women's contributions to the realm of side-show and supporting cast. Medals and recognition follow traditional rules – and there is still an uncomfortable feeling about including auxiliary and civilian efforts on war memorials.

Distinguishing historical truth from exciting myth is made all the harder by the fact that the battlefield is the source of many an inflated story, and both victory and defeat produce tales to excuse the excesses of all sides. Sheer necessity must have dictated circumstances in which a number of aristocratic women led men to war: their rank and position marked them out as automatic leaders, frequently in default of a suitable male. Hierarchy gave them power, and the advantages of education lent them authority. Religion added the dimension of inspiration – especially when virginity was added to the menu of leadership virtues: to have foresworn the usual role of womanhood could be seen as adding strength and confirming that 'no ordinary woman' was taking up the sword. Joan of Arc was variously described by commentators as 'above sex', thus entering a state which qualified her for a military role. And the concept of the Virgin Queen was a powerful image which set Elizabeth I apart and aloof from the usual dependency on male power.

At the level of ordinary soldier, the presence of fighting women can usually be detected by laws forbidding their inclusion in armies. From pre-Roman Celtic gatherings to the English Civil War come mutterings against those who would relinquish the domestic role and join the fight.

What history usually fails to record or recall is the non-heroic side of war: those who cooked, cleaned, supplied, did the washing, tended the wounded and comforted the warriors. Baggage-trains and camp-followers, battlefield scavengers, wives and tarts. An army is a hungry and demanding beast, its commander forever being quoted about its appetite. Marching on its stomach, Napoleon is thought to have said; going on its belly like a serpent, according to Frederick the Great of Prussia. Never mind invasion and battles, an army needs food and drink in order to stay together and be prepared. In the colourful account of the adventures of 'Mother Ross' at the end of the seventeenth century, somewhat embellished by the author Daniel Defoe, the daily task of foraging undertaken by the advance party of camp-followers in Flanders is minutely described:

> I put the carcass of the sheep [which she had just found and killed] on my mare, the fowls I hung about my neck; drove my sheep before me, and so marched to the place designed for the camp, called Havre . . . I pitched my tent near a deserted public house, allotted for Colonel Hamilton's quarters; turned my sheep out to grass and hung up my mutton on a tree to cool: I then went to the Colonel's quarters, over which as soon as it was appointed a guard was set; but by a bribe, I struck him so blind, that he could not see me and my husband's comrades, who lent a friendly hand, carry off a large quantity of faggots, hay and straw for my mare, and my own bed; fill all my empty flasks with beer, and roll off a whole barrel to my tent . . . I made four crowns a-piece of my sheep, besides the fat, which I sold to a woman who made mould candles for the men, and made a good penny of my fowls and pigeons.

Mother Ross, or Kit Davies or Christian Welch or Mrs Christian

Ross or Mrs Jones – she had four husbands – was celebrated by Defoe in his account of her life as a soldier 'who in several campaigns under King William and the late Duke of Marlborough, in the quality of a Foot Soldier and Dragoon gave many signal Proofs of an unparallell'd Courage and personal Bravery'. Born in Dublin, she inherited a pub from her aunt, married her servant Richard Welch and bore him three children. One night he disappeared, and a year later a letter arrived from Holland explaining that he'd been press-ganged into the army after being carried aboard a ship dead drunk. Twenty-six years old, she set off to find him: 'I cut off my hair and dressed me in suit of my husband's having had the precaution to quilt the waistcoat to preserve my breasts from hurt which were not large enough to betray my sex and putting on the wig and hat I had prepared I went out an bought me a silver hilted sword and some Holland shirts.' That a mere change of dress should deceive all and sundry was not so incredible at a time when skirt and breeches were never considered interchangeable between the sexes: you wore a man's clothes – you were assumed to be a man.

Kit joined an infantry regiment and over the years took part in numerous battles: 'We spared nothing, killing, burning, or otherwise destroying whatever we could not carry off. The bells of the churches we broke to pieces, that we might bring them away with us. I filled two bed-ticks, after having thrown out the feathers, with bell-metal, men's and women's clothes, some velvets and about a hundred Dutch caps, which I had plundered from a shop; all of which I sold by the lump to a Jew, who followed the army to purchase our pillage, for four pistoles.' After fighting at Blenheim she finally discovered her husband, but continued to serve at his side until she was seriously wounded at the battle of Ramillies in 1705. At that point, common to many who lived a life in disguise, the game was up when her injuries needed attention. The surgeons informed the commanding officer of the Scots Regiment of White Horses that the 'pretty dragoon' was a woman.

Unfazed, the CO supervised a second wedding in front of the

military, insisting that she resume marital relations with her husband – until then she'd avoided sex for fear that pregnancy would reveal her deceit. Out of uniform, Kit took up full-time occupation as a sutler, providing the army with food and drink and indulging in a great deal of profitable foraging. She was granted a privileged place ahead of the army, rather than with the followers to the rear, though it was still a risky business as she bargained or plundered her way between her own troops and the enemy, loading her mare with beef, butter and bacon: 'Which I had scarcely done when I heard the signal gun, an alarm given the foragers, that the whole body of the enemy was coming upon us; and that their seeming to march to the left, was only to cover the filing of their infantry into the woods. The terror with which the foragers were struck at the news is hardly credible! The fields were strewn with corn, hay and utensils, which they had not the courage to take along with them.'

Until the end of Marlborough's campaigns, in 1712, several children and husbands decorated her life. She was an ambiguous figure, both harassed by randy soldiers and respected by the Duke himself, who said he would as soon take her advice as that of any brigadier in the army. Celebrated in story and ballad, she received a shilling a day pension for life from Queen Anne, ending her days as an out-pensioner at the Royal Hospital in Chelsea.

Other women were alongside Kit Ross on her travels, and her ilk were common on the battlefield until well into the nineteenth century. Sutleresses, sometimes known as *vivandières* and *cantinières*, came to acquire semi-official recognition, and often wore the jackets of the regiments they accompanied. Wives were not uncommon, for campaigns could last for years, and families often had no choice but to follow the flag. Also the army needed seamstresses, cooks and billet organisers, and someone to nurse the wounded. And then there were the women who made a reasonable living from prostitution, who often had a vague claim to be 'nurses'. Not unexpectedly, the character of the camp-following was regarded by many outsiders as something of a rabble of tarts, profiteers and corpse-thieves. But they were necessary, and anyway, the armies they supported were hardly of high moral character and models of propriety.

So why join this motley band as a soldier? The reasons given have always tended to be based on the standard theme of 'following a soldier', and indeed there are many well-documented cases where the search for a husband, or the desire to follow a fiancé or lover, was clearly the over-riding motive. Women who were on their own were in a vulnerable position in society and had little social status.

In 1743, during the War of Austrian Succession, George II became the last British king to command his army personally in battle, at Dettingen. He was probably unaware that one of his dragoons was Mary Ralphson, known as Trooper Mary. Her husband Ralph was in the 3rd Dragoons, and she had accompanied him from Scotland on the campaign only to find herself amid the fighting, whereupon she 'equipped herself in the uniform and accoutrements of a Dragoon who fell wounded by her side, mounted his charger and regained the battle line'. Having had a taste of fighting, she was seen on the field at both Fontenoy and Culloden. Somewhere in the fray at Fontenoy was Phoebe Hassel (or Hessel), who was slashed in the arm by a bayonet and who, according to popular stories, had been serving in the 5th Regiment of Foot ever since her father had enlisted her as a fife player.

Sheer survival could also bring women shoulder to shoulder with men in battle. Much celebrated in Holland was Kenau Haaselaer, a widow who led a tenth of the fighting force, thought to number three hundred women, against the Spanish at the siege of Haarlem in 1572: 'women who fought with manly passion both inside and outside the walls'. In the mid-seventeenth century the English Civil War saw a number of noblewomen leading the defence of their castles and manors, while their humbler sisters were spotted among the Scots soldiers marching on Newcastle: 'women who stood with blue caps among the men'. They cannot have been the only ones, for King Charles I was moved to issue a proclamation which banned women in armies from wearing men's clothing.

Memoirs, popular ballads, stage plays and novels all commemorated female soldiers, and military reports often carried confirmation that the dead on the battlefield included a number of women. Not such a number as to warrant significance, not so few as to be rare birds.

Joining up as an act of female rebellion seems much less common – if at all acknowledged. What is common to many of the women who were discovered to have disguised themselves as sailors and soldiers is their discovery of the 'freedom' which wearing breeches gave them. Those who told their stories after their spell of service all emphasise the extraordinary moment when they were free of their skirts. It was not only freedom of movement that was gained, but the freedom to act very differently. And not just in the social context – joining the men in public places, drinking, perhaps smoking and swearing – but in the sense of being expected to take decisions and act independently without reference to another male, and being accorded respect just for being a man.

Modern terminology would suggest 'empowerment', but it was the mere taste of not being the dependent, subservient sex that often gave these women a reason to continue with their venture into a hard and rigidly masculine world. Clothing delineated one's sex in an inflexible manner, right into the twentieth century. Just the suggestion of 'maids in breeches' was so upsetting that the phrase was only permissible when applied to the stage. Long hair, frilly headwear, petticoats and then corsets – in the general population there was never any doubt about gender as defined by clothes. Even the poorest women had flannel petticoats and a shawl, and were definably woman-shaped. So stepping out of these garments was a revolutionary act, either of defiance or of experiment. Cutting one's hair was another.

Women-as-soldiers also got paid – irregularly at times, and sometimes only with the spoils of war, but the potential for earning more than a pittance as an unskilled single woman was enticing. And then there was the status of being 'a man'. Women with no education discovered that there was a different way of seeing the world – and being seen by it. The main penalty was isolation, and the inability to share both physical space and thoughts and feelings without revealing too much. Relationships? In the public's eyes, the complication of sexual involvement was usually thought to be confined to falling in love with a male soldier. Sexual complications and notions of homosexuality were not part of the perceived situation, and gender confusion or uncertainty were not contemporary preoccupations. 'Cross-dressing' had not been invented as a social issue to be studied, and the psychological aspects of desiring to wear male attire and to take up a wholly masculine line of work were yet to be discovered. These women were seen not as 'deviant', but as 'different'.

Nevertheless, throughout the seventeenth and eighteenth centuries there was public fascination with the women who were revealed as having fought alongside men: they were popular, and they were seen as 'adventuresses'; and although they represented a threat to the conventional order of things, they were on the whole cheered on for having had the audacity to act 'the man'. Those who went to sea were thought particularly dashing, for concealment there, in the confines of a ship, was even harder. Lady pirates such as Anne Bonney and Mary Read were absorbed into folklore in their own lifetimes. Many other women, such as Mary Ann Talbot, were reported as serving on naval ships of the line, their sex only revealed when captured or injured. Mary Ann retired on a pension of £20 a year granted for 'wounds received in action'.

Hannah Snell too was awarded a pension, having served briefly in the army, deserted, then headed for Portsmouth and enlisted in Colonel Fraser's Regiment of Marines. She led a colourful life, enhanced by an equally colourful biography entitled *The Female Soldier; or the Surprising Life and Adventures of Hannah Snell*. There was much that was surprising therein, including a description of being wounded at the siege of Pondicherry in India (six shots in the right leg, seven in the left, and another in the groin). Hannah maintained that she concealed her sex by extracting the musket ball in her groin herself 'with thumb and finger'. Whatever the authenticity of detail in her life, there's no doubting the entry in the admission book in the Royal Hospital, Chelsea, where she was admitted as an out-pensioner: 'Wounded at Pondicherry in the thigh of both legs, born at Worcester, her father a dyer.'

However, also aboard before Victorian times were quite a female crew: wives, seamstresses and cooks sailed with the Royal Navy, and Nelson's fleet had skirts below decks during many encounters. At the battle of the Nile John Nichol was one of the gun crew on the *Goliath* off Alexandria:

> The sun was just setting as we went into the bay, and a red and fiery sun it was. I would, if I had had my choice, been on the deck; there I would have seen what was passing, and the time would not have hung so heavy; but every man does his duty with spirit, whether his station be in the slaughter-house or in the magazine. (The seamen call the lower deck, near the main-mast, 'the slaughter-house', as it is amidships, and the enemy aim their fire principally at the body of the ship.) My station was in the powder-magazine with the gunner. As we entered the bay we stripped to our trousers, opened our ports, cleared, and every ship we passed gave them a broadside and three cheers. Any information we got was from the boys and women who carried the powder. They behaved as well as the men, and got a present for their bravery from the Grand Signior. When the French Admiral's ship blew up, the Goliath got such a shake we thought the after-part of her had blown up until the boys told us what it was. They brought us every now and then the news of another French ship having struck, and we answered the cheers on deck with heartfelt joy. In the heat of the action, a shot came right into the magazine, but did no harm, as the carpenters plugged it up, and stopped the water that was rushing in. I was much

indebted to the gunner's wife, who gave her husband and me a drink of wine every now and then, which lessened our fatigue much. There were some women wounded, and one woman belonging to Leith died of her wounds, and was buried on a small island in the bay. One woman bore a son in the heat of the action; she belonged to Edinburgh.

The most curious case is that of Dr Barry, who rose to the top of the Army's medical service with a rank equivalent to major-general. From his sudden appearance in 1809 as James Barry, a medical student at Edinburgh University, through his demanding and distinguished career as an army surgeon and medical inspector, to his final post as the senior of Her Majesty's Inspectors General of Hospitals, he was regarded as a trifle 'effeminate', being a beardless five-foot eccentric. His uniform was always exquisite – sword and plumed hat and exaggeratedly padded jacket – and he had a toy dog in attendance. His medical skills were admired, he dealt with Florence Nightingale during the Crimean War, and he spent forty-six years in the army. When he died in 1865 in London, the death certificate registered him as a male. But the keener eyes of the woman laying out the body knew what she was looking at: Dr Barry was 'a perfect female', and more-over had 'had a child when very young'.

Dr Barry must inevitably have felt isolated at times. It was only in the year of his death that Elizabeth Garrett Anderson passed her Apothecaries' Examination, on her way to becoming Britain's first practising woman doctor. And the army – rather more keenly than the rest of society – still saw medical matters as a male pursuit, especially where soldiers were concerned. Mid-Victorian England had also shifted public attitudes to the ideal female towards a creature who had the vapours and who was politely ignorant of anatomical details. Even when it came to nursing, the Queen's army had adopted a position of priggish hostility to the women who traditionally followed the flag.

Women have always nursed the wounded – but their proximity

to the battlefield has depended on society's view of their vulnerability or their status. In Afghanistan, even as late as the 1980s, a woman wrapped in a blue *burkah* described her helplessness to me after her husband was injured by a land-mine during the Soviet invasion.

'He's lost an eye and an leg,' she said. 'He lay bleeding for hours in our fields, because I couldn't go to him. It wasn't allowed – it's Islam. We women had to stay in our quarters whatever happened. So he was nearly dead when he was brought in. I feel it's my fault – a woman should be able to help even if you have to go into a minefield.'

Nevertheless, for centuries soldiers were lucky if they received any medical care at all. As there was little enough interest taken in keeping them healthy when not actually fighting, there was even less when they met a bullet or a bayonet. The rag-tag baggage-train which accumulated round any army might have a few motherly souls prepared to tend injuries; but designated 'nurses' were not to be found among the wives, sutlers, *vivandières*, washer-women, seamstresses and whores who otherwise sustained a successful campaign. Nursing was the province of the religious. And nuns and baggage-trains were mutually exclusive. However, it was the fusion of a saintly image with militaristic discipline which laid the foundations of modern nursing.

Aged sixteen, Florence Nightingale wrote that 'God spoke to me and called me to His service', though it was many years before she knew exactly what she was meant to achieve. However, for a well-brought-up middle-class young lady in the 1840s she showed an unconventional interest in hospitals. Her family and friends were perfectly normal in indulging in Victorian fits of the vapours as Florence began to tour wards, develop a fascination with drains, and read official reports on the Sanitary Condition of the Labouring Classes. Hospitals were vile places. They stank, they were verminous, their walls and floors and ceilings were coated with putrid matter, and they were unquiet: drink and madness saw to that, with the police having to sort out disturbances among the tightly packed beds in the half-dark. The staff drank, too. And nurses were in many instances synonymous with prostitutes. 'It was *preferred*', wrote Florence, 'that the nurses should be women who had lost their characters, i.e. should have had one child.' But salvation, in the form of the Institution of Kaiserswerth on the Rhine for the Practical Training of Deaconesses, came in 1851, and so began the extraordinary labours which led to one woman revolutionising the role of the nurse – and also the image.

When Miss Nightingale's nurses set off three years later for the appalling hospitals on the shores of the Bosphorus, where the British army was losing more men to disease than to battle during the Crimean War, they were not a bevy of crisply uniformed ministering angels. Admittedly, twenty-four came from religious institutions, almost wholly interested in the patient's soul and distinctly indifferent to his body, especially the parts that were either intimate or dirty: flitting about like angels without hands, was Florence's judgement on them. The other fourteen described themselves as nurses, and were best described as the least worst of those who presented themselves for interview. All were well past their prime, which subsequently led to a letter from 'The Bird', as Florence became widely known, in which she stated that in future 'fat drunken old dames of fourteen stones and over must be barred, the provision of bedsteads is not strong enough'. However, all had been provided with a uniform, which in the glorious tradition of uniforms did not actually fit: the result was fourteen women of assorted size in a grey tweed dress, grey worsted jacket, plain white cap, short woollen cloak and 'a frightful scarf of brown, with the words Scutari Hospital embroidered in red'. Though not an ideal uniform, it served the Nightingale purpose of delineating the nurse from the casual camp-follower, yet avoided imitating the nuns; the short cloak appears to have been the forerunner of the distinctive red cape still worn by British military nurses today.

The hell that was Scutari tested everything that nursing would ever be faced with. The Barrack Hospital sat on a cesspool; mud, muck and mighty rats were everywhere, and the odd dead horse turned up in rubbish heaps. Supplies were badly administered, stolen or non-existent. The injured came in a never-ending stream. The nurses endured dreadful conditions – the first party of Anglican nuns found their bedroom occupied by a recently expired Russian general. The doctors were suspicious to the point of hostility to nursing sisters. Paperwork dominated while patients died. Religion and class both raised their heads as the purpose and form of a nursing service went though its birth pangs.

Who should do the cleaning? Who runs a hospital – medics or managers? Who holds the purse-strings? Is it a vocation to scrub floors – and earn a pittance? What's the status of a nurse? Even the Crimea had its quota of fraightfully naice ladies who deemed a smile and a few pious words more appropriate than a scrubbing brush and a blood-spattered apron. Over the decades after the Crimea, Florence Nightingale planned, plotted, badgered and campaigned. What emerged, in both the training and ethos – even in the uniforms – was a secular and civilian service, but one which was rooted in religious tradition and military discipline.

Curiously, she never wore uniform. Popular pictures of 'The Lady with the Lamp' were nearly all the product of artists' imaginations, and some of them show a small but elegant figure walking the grim hospital wards in tight corset and swishing crinoline skirt as worn by every fashionable woman in the 1850s. The crinoline was a cage of whalebone or wire, or hoops of steel springs, so unwieldy that precious ornaments, table lamps and small children could be knocked for six if the wearer twirled unexpectedly. Miss Nightingale had no truck with such frippery, writing that 'a respectable elderly woman stooping forward, invested in the crinoline, exposes quite as much of her own person to the patient lying in the room as any opera-dancer on stage.' However, though she also thought the sound of 'rattling stays' disturbed the sick, her list of requirements addressed 'To the Nurses about to join the Army Hospitals in the East' included among the Flannel Petticoats and the Upper Petticoats a Pair of Stays.

It's fairly certain that her own dress was usually black, trimmed with white collar and cuffs, accompanied by the small cap worn by all Victorian ladies. Not consciously a uniform – but one which survives in those few hospitals today where Matron still rules.

The nurses were all civilians, and therefore did not qualify for any military decorations. In 1855 Miss Nightingale was presented by Queen Victoria with a jewel designed by Prince Albert: the cross of St George bearing the word 'Crimea', surmounted with a diamond crown. The lady nurses were each given a circular gold brooch, enamelled in red and green, with a diamond crescent in the centre – not from the Queen but from the Sultan of Turkey, who sent a sum of money to the British government to pay for them.

By the turn of the century, notwithstanding the reservations of die-hard army officers about loose-moralled hangers-on in the wards, the Nightingale influence was worldwide. Training schools flourished, women had joined the staff of military hospitals, and the American Civil War had found Dorothea Dix as Superintendent of Women Nurses confronting and overcoming the same prejudices as had existed in the Crimea, and Clara Barton gaining fame and admiration through working on the actual battlefield. The status of the profession had risen.

Grumble as they might, forty years later in South Africa at the time of the Boer War the British officers, seeing their men plagued by dust, flies, bugs and fleas, were soon faced with the familiar statistic that more of them were being carried off by dysentery and cholera than were being shot by the enemy. The services of over fifteen hundred army nurses – working well away from the battle zone in military hospitals – were deemed a necessity. Nevertheless, there were still many prejudices to overcome. Far from being allowed to hover with their lamps over the beds of wounded soldiers at night, the nurses were shunted off to their quarters at sunset and only gained access to the hospital wards if summoned and given a military escort. Lurking in the military mind was a centuries-old suspicion that women who hung around beds were up to no good. Added to that, the senior army surgeon had made it perfectly clear that he didn't approve of 'lady nurses' in any circumstances. And then there were the social butterflies of Cape Town. Once again, the professional nursing staff found themselves up against the ladies 'who dispensed smiles and visits', giving rise to an early version of a long-standing hospital joke: from a military hospital in the Cape Province came the story of the patient besieged by nursing do-gooders, who eventually wrote a card to hang above his bed: 'I am too ill to be nursed today.' I last heard this going the rounds in Belgium, in a hospital full of survivors from the Zeebrugge ferry disaster in 1987; the Prince and Princess of Wales had just beaten the Prime Minister to the main ward, whereupon a patient was reported as having pasted on his bed-head a notice reading: 'Too exhausted to be visited by Mrs Thatcher.'

The Boer War gave impetus to the formal establishment of Queen Alexandra's Imperial Military Nursing Service in 1902, for the first time recognising these women as members of the forces rather than regarding them as civilians; even so, they were technically 'in' the army, but not 'of' it. The uniform was a long grey dress covered by a white apron, with floaty white veil and scarlet cape approved by the Queen herself – who was a stylish Dane. That the effect should be both distinctive and elegant was a necessary factor in a society where clothes spelled status, and upper-class women spent a good deal of time with their maid heaving on the strings of the newly fashionable S-shaped corset, aiming for a tiny waist between low bosom and humpy hips. In formal photographs, the newly militarised QAs display enviably nipped-in waistlines, attesting to the powerful presence of whalebone beneath, but at least they had only a few variations to their basic uniform for different formal functions; society *grandes dames* changed up to six times a day. As for practicality, skirts were still full and long, the cap-strings were fiddly, and corsets have never been comfortable. However, the desired effect was achieved: striking, stylish and respectable.

It took decades for Victorian women to establish their presence as nurses amidst Britain's military operations, and the perfectly dressed military surgeon Dr Barry had taken it for granted that he'd be the sole female soldier on a battlefield. However, just as he came to the end of his extraordinary career in 1862, newspapers were carrying numerous reports of the American Civil War in which instances of women's participation as would-be combatants were so frequent that they merited scant attention. Several hundred women appear to have been discovered through injury or death, others were surprised by their male colleagues and discharged, and yet more seem to have made it through the war undetected. The *Harrisburg Patriot* reported from a local army camp in 1861:

On Monday afternoon two gentlemen – solid-looking farmers – arrived in Camp Curtin, who sought an interview with the officer of the day, and informed him that they were in search of a girl who had strayed away. The officer thought a military camp a queer place to hunt for stray girls, especially as it reflected on the virtue and dignity of the men at arms, nevertheless the gentlemen were at liberty to make a search. As the old song says, 'they hunted her high and they hunted her low,' but they did not hunt her 'when a year had passed away,' for lo! In less than an hour she was found on guard doing duty as a sentinel, in the uniform of Capt. Kuhn's company of Sumner Rifles, of Carlisle – We do not know what name she enlisted under to protect the honor of her country's flag, but her real name is Sophia Cryder, and her residence only about a mile from this city. She had been in Capt. Kuhn's company a week, is a plump lass of only sixteen years of age, and had so completely unsexed herself that she could safely bid defiance to any one not acquainted with her to detect her. How she shirked an examination, which is said to be made with great strictness by the medical men of Camp Curtin, we are not informed.

She is represented as a girl of unblemished reputation, and did not, as generally happens in such cases, enlist to be near the object of her affections, but merely in a wild spirit of adventure. It does not speak well for the modesty of Miss Sophia, however, to say, that she was in the habit of accompanying the men on their excursions to the river to bathe; but she may have done this to ward off suspicion especially as she took precious good care to keep out of the water herself. This is the first case of the kind that has been brought to light, but we are informed that the most reckless dare-devil attached to the Seventh regiment of the three month's volunteers was a woman – *mother of four children.*

Miss Cryder was taken home, where she can reflect over what she did not see.

The following year the *Semi-Weekly Dispatch* reported the enlisting in the 107th Pennsylvania Regiment of an eighteen-year-old boy who 'bore a softened and pleasing expression'. The other recruits thought he had better

conquer his timidity before he could be considered a man and a soldier. The young recruit, however, soon undeceived them, and he could smoke a cigar, swagger, and take an occasional 'horn' with the most perfect sang froid . . . The regiment finally departed for Washington, and we lose sight of our recruit until within the last week or so, when his reappearance was hailed with some surprise by several officers of a recruiting station in this place. He gave no explanation of the reason for his return, but it has been ascertained, since reaching home, that he has abandoned male attire, donned petticoats and frock, and is a girl again! She says she is determined 'to try it again'.

Comparing such women to Joan of Arc and Edward III's queen,

Philippa, the *Semi-Weekly Dispatch* felt that they were being wrongly overlooked:

> The same love of country and desire for fame actuate our female volunteers, who don male attire and present themselves at the various recruiting stations in the North for enlistment. In most cases their sex has not been known at the time of enlistment, but in every case, as far as we know, after reaching the seat of war, the poor, proscribed sex of these candidates for military glory has been discovered, and they have been returned to the obscurity of their former life.

Concealment was made easier by the non-standard array of clothing which was the lot of the ordinary soldier. For centuries, battlefields had been colourful and confusing: loyalty, fashion, hierarchy, pride and practicality all fought for consideration in the matter of uniforms. Artists frequently depicted orderly encounters in which colour and style easily defined friend and foe, when the reality was a kaleidoscope of individualistic tradition. Mercenaries, bodyguards, privately raised regiments, local militias and standing armies all brought their own standards of dress to a war. And the primary function of a uniform's colour had nearly always been to act as a badge of allegiance for the common soldier, rather than to distinguish him from the enemy.

Towards the end of the seventeenth century in Europe, some kind of standardisation began to appear with the rise of permanent or national armies. Even so, once these armies intermingled mistakes were easy. In the early eighteenth century the French – on the whole – wore white, and the Austrians pearl-grey. However, the Austrians had the habit of whitening their coats with pipeclay, leading to an intentional – and successful – muddle, narrated by the French Colonel de la Colonie: 'I became grimly aware of several lines of infantry in greyish-white uniforms on our left flank. I verily believed reinforcements had reached us ... So in the error I laboured under, I shouted to my men that they were

Frenchmen and friends. Having, however, made a closer inspection, I discovered bunches of straw attached to their standards, badges the enemy are in the custom of wearing in battle, but at that very moment was struck in the jaw by a ball that stupefied me.'

Even as nations strove to achieve standardisation internal rivalries between regiments reasserted themselves, fuelled by insistence on arcane traditions and determination to avoid uniformity while dressed in uniform. Anyway, uniforms were intended for show – to show others that you were impressive and proud to declare your allegiance.

So, for women joining up, disguise was not too difficult. Added to this, armies were chaotic and mobile, and concealment could be effected in a heaving mass of unregistered fighters. Medical examinations were usually cursory, and anyway, there were other women around in the baggage-train. However, in the nineteenth century, as the Victorians began to build barracks for a standing army and to introduce a much more regulated life for a soldier, the women began to be edged out. Camp-followers were gradually replaced by army-run support systems. The useful rabble was made redundant. Garrison towns operated rules and regulations, and the services began to take an official interest in running soldiers' private lives. And in the navy, the call to 'show a leg' was no longer relevant: the habit of having women stay on board while ships were in port was ending. Seamen would no longer be allowed an extra hour's snooze if a hairless leg was shown to the bosun's mate on his rounds, for the ladies were now being turfed out of their hammocks for good. The military was becoming a world apart, entirely male, and not so interwoven with its supporters and relatives – and its women.

And the military were beginning to *look* a world apart: the common soldiers were starting to appear uniform in their uniforms, and the officers were turning into peacocks. In the nineteenth century gold braid and copious frogging, feathers and fur, tight breeches and elegant boots all made their way into various

European uniforms; sex appeal arrived as well, for showy plumage called attention to a profession which stood for manliness and adventure, a masculine approach to life and a slightly monastic existence in barracks and mess and club. Women were meant to admire – but that was all.

Even so, by mid-century serviceable khaki had been adopted by the British in India and another fifty years saw the entire army clad in 'dust colour'. Elsewhere in Europe, however, right up to the early days of World War I it was still possible to find gorgeous colours and showy outfits, to the detriment, for instance, of the ordinary French soldiers who faced German machine-gunners in 1914 while wearing their traditional, highly visible scarlet trousers.

Meanwhile, in the twentieth century the military had discovered once again that it needed the services of women. It reinvented the baggage-train and camp-followers, but this time in uniform.

CHAPTER TWO

DASHINGLY TO WAR

'YOU KNOW WHAT she's like – she was a fenny, you know.' Grown-ups speak in riddles, and as a child I wondered what the raised eyebrows and shrugged shoulders beneath the hats of the Conservative Party Tea Club meant. When I was a little older, but none the wiser, the word appeared again – this time in an announcement by a particularly stuck-up but dim school prefect: 'Well, my auntie was a fanny, so she was *very* important in the war.' The mysterious word had altered slightly in pronunciation – and we suggestible teenage girls suppressed giggles as we guessed at its possible meaning.

The First Aid Nursing Yeomanry was not part of our lives. World War I was in the far distance. Indeed, World War II had happened before we were born, and we were not part of the *Boys' Own* world which consumed Biggles or How to Escape from Stalag Luft III or Instructions for Building Your Own Miniature Submarine. Uniforms had been put away by our parents' generation and Civvy Street embraced, and the phrases such as 'Can I do you now, sir?', which left adults shaking with laughter from memories of wit on the wireless, belonged firmly to an incomprehensible period. But with two generations still alive that had seen two world wars, phrases and habits died hard. And the certain something about a FANY lingered on, and seemed to be rather envied.

The organisation appeared to have slightly romantic roots: Sergeant-Major Edward Charles Baker was a British cavalryman who'd been wounded while fighting in the campaign in the Sudan at the end of the nineteenth century, and he dreamed up – perhaps he dreamed about – a unit of ladies on horseback, riding with the skirmishing parties and swooping down upon the field of battle to carry injured men to safety. How he presented this idea to stolid Edwardian army types is not clear, but in 1907, having left the army and while working for the Armour Meat Packing Company at Smithfield Market, he managed to form a group of mounted auxiliaries to the Royal Army Medical Corps, some of whom were nurses. In his newspaper advertisement for recruits he'd stated: 'Our mission is to tend Britain's soldiers on the field and prove ourselves worthy country-women of the first and greatest of Britain's army nurses' (the eighty-seven-year-old Florence Nightingale had just been awarded the Order of Merit by King Edward VII – the first time it had been given to a woman).

From the very start they had a certain air about them; first aid allied with horsemanship added up to An Accomplishment, something a nicely brought-up gel might acquire, and so the first-ever officially recognised uniformed women's service was born. The ladies were turned out smartly, perched decorously side-saddle in dark blue riding skirts with a striking military-style scarlet tunic and cap, though they soon adopted khaki for the skirt and swapped the cap for a topee – a tropical sun helmet.

According to an article in the *Daily Graphic* on 25 February 1909:

A mere male member of the *Daily Graphic* staff yesterday invaded the sanctum of the First Aid Nursing Yeomanry Corps in Holborn. On giving the password to the pretty sentinel on duty at the door, he found himself in the presence of a busy band of aristocratic amazons in arms. Their purpose was peaceful. In their picturesque uniforms, they were engaged in recruiting work. There was a constant stream of Lady callers, most of them Society folk, whose patriotism had impelled them to enrol in the Corps which is being formed to enable women to help their country in wartime. Surrounded by gaily garbed sergeants and corporals, Lady Ernestine Hunt, the eldest daughter of the Marquis of Aylesbury, who looked dashing in her uniform of scarlet tunic and dark skirt relieved with white braid, was hard at work.

Miss Grace Ashley-Smith was an early recruit. A Scot from Aberdeen and a first-class horsewoman (ladies with their own horses were particularly sought after), she wrote a training manual and recruited vigorously:

I hunted round for recruits and pestered all my friends to join. That was the first step. The second was to weed out others, amongst them a soulful lady with peroxide hair, very fat and hearty, who insisted on wearing white drawers with frills under her khaki skirt. She also insisted on falling off at every parade and displaying them. She was so breezy and warm-hearted that it cost me a pang, but she had to go; no woman's movement could have survived those white frilly drawers on parade.

In 1909 there were about a hundred members of the Corps, and Sergeant-Major Baker had promoted himself to the honorary rank of captain. The women had to undergo a course in first aid and home nursing, horsemanship, veterinary work, signalling and camp cookery – and provide their own uniforms. They took part in military tattoos and paraded with their horse ambulance before graduating to riding astride – a rather thrilling innovation which saw them wearing a button-through khaki skirt which divided to reveal a pair of elegant breeches. There was an annual camp, again remarkable for the fact that women were living under canvas, just like the military. However it's unlikely the military would have recognised the activities: 'Hunting for Casualties' and 'Wounded Rescue Races'.

Interviewing some of the original members for a history of the unit, Dame Irene Ward recorded one of them saying that 'We were stared at so much, that you simply had to have a sense of humour to carry on.' And they were sometimes mistaken for suffragettes – once, in London's Tottenham Court Road, a crowd of thirty factory girls started booing and shouting, throwing things and calling, 'You———— suffragettes!' Then one pointed to her Red Cross badge on her sleeve: 'You would not believe the sudden silence, the shame-faced Sorrys and the melting away of those girls in less than 2 minutes.' A Miss Bannatyne remembered:

> As to the general public, when they first caught sight of us, they just did not know what we were, and every body stared in amazement, and it took some courage to walk or bus by ourselves. At times we felt like freaks. But it was not long before the Press started writing about us and putting up photos of which there were plenty. . . . I have even had sentries on duty and soldiers in the street, when they saw my pips, give me, or rather the uniform, a salute and very gravely I would return it.

Nursing was a tough, disciplined business, thanks to the Nightingale legacy, and it's not surprising that there seems to have been no formal link between the military nurses and the Edwardian ladies who joined the FANY in the first decade of the twentieth century. The image of rather well-bred ladies dashing about the battlefield on horseback sat ill with trained nurses encouraged to see their work as a vocation. Nor did the FANY appeal to another determined woman who felt that 'women could do things which tradition had supposed they were incapable'.

Mabel Annie Stobart was an adventurous character who'd spent part of her life in the African veldt and in British Columbia. Not in the suffrage movements, but claiming to be a 'feminist' – describing her husband as a 'masculinist' – she had her inspiration in 1909. This was a year when there'd been widespread fear in Britain that a German invasion was imminent, and while the Votes for Women movement was demanding a share in government, Mrs Stobart thought that this should be complemented by women taking a share in the defence of their country. She'd seen a popular play in London by Guy du Maurier called *An Englishman's Home*, and though unimpressed by its theatrical qualities ('crude, inartistic, melodramatic and far-fetched' – Mrs Stobart was not one to mince words) she pondered its theme:

An Englishman's home was invaded by the enemy and women could do nothing even to staunch the wounds of their men-folk. I forget the details. But I asked myself what could *I* have done? What could all those 'Votes for Women' claimants have done? What was there we could do or should be allowed to do in case of foreign invasion? I found that, in schemes of defence, no provision was made for the help of women. A great deal has been made of Florence Nightingale's victory, but its present-day results were small, and only, at the best, affected trained hospital nurses.

Galloping round Hyde Park with the FANY didn't seem the right answer to Mrs Stobart. She joined for a short time; but it was too fanciful for words, in her view. So the Women's Sick and Wounded Convoy Corps was born – and got several years' training under its belt in moving casualties from the front clearing stations to hospitals in the rear. In 1912 it went to the aid of the Bulgarian army in the Balkan War, and two years later, on the first day of World War I, Mrs Stobart went into action again. She'd been at a meeting attended by many prominent suffrage campaigners in Kingsway Hall in London. She was asked what she intended to do. There and then she decided to form women's units 'to do women's work of relieving the suffering of sick and wounded, or of any other service that might be required'.

They may have worn grand feathered hats and sweeping skirts, but the women who felt the need for action in 1914 had been pushing against convention for many years. The suffrage question was being debated from America to China and there was growing agitation in many countries for improved education and employment opportunities for women. Those who found themselves on the springboard at the outbreak of war, like Mrs Stobart and the FANY, had experienced skirmishing in the undergrowth of discrimination and inequality. Nevertheless, across Europe the majority of women were still untouched by radical ideas, none more so than the woman who was quintessentially a put-upon wife and second-class citizen but whose death initiated profound change for millions.

CHAPTER THREE

SARAJEVO: A BULLET THROUGH THE CORSET

YOU'RE SITTING IN a bone-rattling car on a hot day in June, the whalebone corset pinching under your elegant gown. There's been a bit of a scene at the town hall in Sarajevo, and your husband – a difficult man at the best of times – has been furious and rude to everyone. Yet again, you've had to calm him down. Lunch at the town hall has been slightly tedious, and you've spent rather a long time upstairs making pointless small talk with a group of ladies in their quaint national costumes – while listening to your husband barking at officials below: he apparently didn't think much of a welcome which included a man throwing a bomb at your car on the way to lunch.

Rather abruptly, you find yourself emerging into the sunshine and putting on the expected smile for a man with one of those new-fangled film cameras before getting back into the open car – a bit nervous now, and your husband still grumpy. Your corset is digging in, and your husband is taking up much of the seat in his bulky uniform. You ought to be wearing uniform too – but they say you're not grand enough, not the 'right' sort of person. And so you're off to make history and to become the first person to die in the War to End All Wars – even though you're not in uniform . . .

The Archduchess Sophie with her husband Franz Ferdinand, heir to the throne of the Austro-Hungarian Empire, bowled along the riverside road. Drawing level with a stone bridge, their driver was confused about the route. A Serb student, Gavrilo Princip, stepped forward and fired two shots, killing both of them; Sophie herself died within seconds. Yet her death is mentioned as an afterthought, an 'also', to the incident in Sarajevo in 1914 when Franz Ferdinand was assassinated, thus precipitating the slaughter of millions. He was the symbol of imperial power and rank; she was the lady in the feathered hat.

Her name, therefore, is not automatically associated with war. She played the role of wife, and the world of politics and the military were closed to her. As a good wife, and Sophie was almost alone in her affection and support for the inadequate and difficult Franz Ferdinand, she dressed the part, did what was expected of her – smiled and waved – and was a loving mother to their two children. In this, she reflected the millions of women who were about to be touched by war.

And yet Sophie in 1914 was more acutely aware than most of her position as a second-class citizen – without a uniform. Her husband, as Inspector General of the army, had been watching the Austrian troops on manoeuvres, and although it had become fashionable for royal ladies to be seen on horseback in dashingly tailored military uniforms, viewing the soldiers as their 'honorary colonel', Sophie had not been awarded this courtesy. Queen

Victoria had begun the trend, described by A.B. Tucker in *Royal Ladies and Soldiers* in 1906:

> In the early days of her reign, the late Queen used, when reviewing her own troops, to wear a military cap edged with gold lace and a blue cloth coat. On the occasion of the inauguration of the Victoria Cross, 50 years ago, Her Majesty wore a round hat with a gold band, and on the right side a red and white feather. Her dress consisted of a scarlet bodice made like a military tunic, but open from the throat. Over her shoulders she wore a gold embroidered sash, while a dark blue skirt completed her costume.

The idea had come from Germany, and among that vast spider's web of inter-related royal families in the nineteenth century there was a raft of queens and grand duchesses and princesses all perched side-saddle on pawing chargers, wearing epaulettes and medals and very glamorous braided tunics. Whether they should have completed the ensemble with the *Pickelhaube* is questionable; the spiked military helmet didn't quite go with the sweeping skirt. Nor did the busby sporting a death's head emblem, as worn by Prussian princesses.

However, Sophie could only dream of such finery, for as the twentieth century began social precedence and rigid convention ruled in Europe, no more so than in the stuffy confines of the Austro-Hungarian court. Being born the Countess Sophie Chotek von Chotkova und Wognin might sound grand, but for the ancient – though rather crumbling – Hapsburgs in Vienna Franz Ferdinand's decision to marry a mere Czech countess from Bohemia had been greeted as if he'd dragged in the local washerwoman. Sophie endured years of exquisite humiliation as she was left out of formal court gatherings, stopped from walking next to her husband in royal processions, put to the back of the queue behind higher-ranking ladies, shunted out of carriages in royal processions, and given a series of niggardly titles culminating in 'Highness, with the qualification of Princely Grace' all of which added up to being addressed as The Not Quite Royal Enough Person. Behind her back, they hissed loudly about '*die böhmische Trampel*' – the Bohemian oik. Her marriage was designated morganatic – in other words, her children would not succeed to the throne. Honorary colonel of a regiment of the great empire? Pretty uniform with epaulettes? Not a chance.

However, the day in Sarajevo had looked quite promising: Bosnia was going to treat them both in a manner that befitted an imperial couple, and Sophie was dressed to the nines when she joined her husband after the morning military display to accompany him into the town. She was a column of delicate pale drapery, cinched with a broad sash to which a large tassel was attached. It's highly unlikely that she had discarded her corset, as 'advanced' ladies had begun to do a few years earlier, following the revolutionary exhortations of the young Paris couturier Paul Poiret. After two children and with a tendency to plumpness, a woman of her class would never have risked such unbecoming behaviour; however, she showed the new shape which was a liberation from the S-bend contortions of the Edwardian era. Her corset would have been long and straight, defining her waist and influencing her stride – straight-backed and slightly stiff. She carried an elegant matching parasol and a delicate handbag, but wore no gloves. No heavy jewellery either, only a gold lorgnette hanging on her fashionably flattish bodice. And a hat which had required the sacrifice of several ostriches. Forty-six years old, and finally beginning to act like a future emperor's wife, Sophie was restrained yet fashionable. Her outfit clearly required the attention of others, and she would not have done much of the dressing herself. Upper-class women had a gaggle of servants – a Lady's maid, for instance, went everywhere with her mistress – and the imperial party occupied the whole of the hotel at Ilidza, just outside Sarajevo. Dressmakers, seamstresses and washerwomen all gained employment from a rich woman's wardrobe, and there was always someone to stick a foot in the small of her back and heave on the corset laces. And despite the recent introduction of more fluid and practical fashions in Paris, formal clothing for the establishment – as ever – would be slow to adapt, so the decorous and sweet pea-coloured figure alighting from an open touring car in front of Sarajevo's town hall fulfilled the expectations of the crowd.

Her husband was in uniform, bulging everywhere, even though he too had the benefit of a corset, the essential accessory for military grandees squeezed into sharply cut tunics. Franz Ferdinand was bedecked with a row of medals, as befitted an archduke, and, hand on sword, sweated under a cocked hat smothered in light green feathers. There was no hint here of the khaki and grey which would fill the fields of Flanders in the coming years. Earlier, the officers round him had glinted and flashed in the Bosnian sunlight, as the show of military brass and scarlet and plumes and swords wheeled past at the manoeuvres. This was what armies were all about. Men with spiked helmets, gold braid and epaulettes. Lively horses with expensive tack, all silver chains and jogging tassels. Thrilling gallops as artillery pieces clattered and flashed around the field. This was 1914, and warfare was paraded as glamorous and manly, a fitting scene for an archduke to view. The archduchess, pointedly, had not been invited.

When the imperial couple met up for their drive to the town hall, small crowds watched the smart cars navigate the narrow Sarajevo streets. The city boasted imposing Hapsburgian buildings, and a number of Turkish confections from its days as part of the Ottoman Empire – mosques and bath-houses, as well as a central bazaar. But much of Bosnia was an imperial backwater, with raw poverty in the mountain villages. Rural life might look picturesque, and the mixture of religions had brought some literacy, but there were also violence and harsh tradition, with women seen as wholly subservient, possessing few legal rights and bearing children year in year out. To the south, in Montenegro and Albania, girls were still sold into a marriage arranged at their birth, leading some foreign travellers to describe them as 'breeding sows'.

The diversity of Bosnia's ethnic mix was caught by the film camera following the royal couple in Sarajevo: a few men in the old Turkish fez, others with heads topped by the traditional white felt plantpot-shaped hat of peasants; women in traditional embroidered Slav costumes or baggy Muslim trousers, with quaint headdresses and clunking jewellery. Many were merely wrapped in layers of dull, flea-infested material, the shawls and headscarves of the poor. The archduchess may have felt second-class in her chiffon and feathers, denied an elegant uniform; but she shared her inferior status, her position of deference and her exclusion from the military with the Bosnian peasant women she was waving to. Even though the century was over a decade old, and women in some European countries were agitating for the vote and beginning to shed their whalebone underwear, much of the professional world was still barred to them, politics belonged to men, and soldiering excluded women. Hundreds of thousands of men were under arms in an increasingly uneasy Europe, but the only women in distinctive uniform were nuns, nurses and nannies. And after the kerfuffle next to the bridge, when she took a fatal shot in the abdomen, Sophie was sent back to Austria to a second-class grave. Her husband's coffin bore all the insignia of the imperial house; on hers were a pair of white gloves and a little fan, and it was carefully laid to rest several inches lower than his.

Three-quarters of a century later, I wondered how the city of Sarajevo remembered the couple. 'There's a small museum,' I was told, right on the corner next to the bridge where the Serb student Gavrilo Princip had taken aim. 'And Tito's regime stuck a plaque on the wall and plonked a pair of metal footprints into the pavement' – so you can stand on them and imagine just what it was like to be a mere six feet from the shiny car, with its grand occupants, and fire the fatal shots.

It was not the best of summers to be a tourist. In 1992 I first spied the old town hall from behind a large metal rubbish skip, which then sprang two small holes with a strange soft pinging sound, as compacted stinking food waste and a couple of dead dogs slowed the bullets' trajectories.

Keeping the town hall in sight, my cameraman and I hurtled behind a low wall, for the town hall was spectacularly on fire. All around us fluttered glowing pieces of paper, with some thick, parchment-like pages curling languidly as they danced down from the second and third storeys. For the town hall had become the Sarajevo University Library, repository of some of the more precious books of the unique culture which had seen Ottoman Turkish Islam put down roots in Orthodox Christian Europe. The pink and beige horizontally striped building on the river-bank now presented a ripe target for the Serbian gunners a couple of hundred yards away. For weeks afterwards, enraged Bosnian Muslims told of conspiracies by the Serbs to destroy their culture deliberately 'with special incendiary bombs'. In reality the old town hall was a sitting duck, and the precautions against fire minimal. Because there were snipers about we failed to get round to the front of the building, to see the steps where the archduchess had waved at the people lining the riverbank road. Bits of the central dome's highly decorated support arches were crashing down on to the mosaic floor. The Sarajevo Fire Brigade made valiant efforts, but arcs of water squirted from the numerous bullet punctures in the hoses and there was little that could be done.

By chance half an hour later, due to random explosions which sent us scuttling – as fast as weighty flak-jackets allowed – down a side street towards the river, we came across the Princip Bridge ahead of us, confirmed by a yellow tourist sign spattered with shrapnel holes. The stone bridge had wonky, ugly modern rail-ings atop two elegant arches, connecting to territory that was still Muslim on the other side of the river, but something of a free-fire zone for the Serbs.

A short crawl down the pavement saw us within a few yards of the museum – and some feet from our noses were little heaps of grit and rubble, where a paving-stone had been. Sure enough, not even front-line gunfire had stopped history being rearranged again in Bosnia. Determined Muslims had crept to the corner and hacked out the Princip footprints; and the wall plaque was peppered with holes. The exact spot where Sophie and Franz Ferdinand had met their deaths in 1914 was now littered with shrapnel and lumps of building, and iced with glass.

Every so often figures skittered between buildings, some in tattered bits of uniform, others merely clutching the ubiquitous AK47 rifle. Men at war. Although in 1992 most of the women were unseen, hidden in the basements, trying to scrape together oddments of food and cook them without the aid of gas or electricity, or constantly creeping on all fours below window level in apartments overlooked by snipers, there was the occasional figure to be seen dashing amongst the ruins: a woman in camouflage with a semi-automatic rifle.

War changes lives, whether or not you fight, but in the intervening years since Sophie Chotek had dreamed of parading in scarlet and gold women have found themselves increasingly putting on uniform. And their endeavour to do so has mirrored the wider change in women's rights.

CHAPTER FOUR

WE THINK YOU OUGHT TO GO

THE DAY AFTER war broke out Mabel Annie Stobart, the assertive founder of the Women's Sick and Wounded Convoy Corps, acquired an office in St James's Street and formed a Foreign Service and a Home Service. The Foreign Service had women doctors, nurses, cooks, interpreters and 'all workers essential for the independent working of a hospital in war'. Recruiting began at once, and the response with regard to both numbers and money was miraculous.

Mrs Stobart went off to see Sir Frederick Treves, chairman of the British Red Cross Society, and – consistent with prevailing attitudes – got squashed. He said that there 'was not work fitted for women in the sphere of war'. She ignored him and immediately left for Belgium and France, setting up a hospital in Brussels for French and Belgian soldiers, under the friendlier auspices of the Belgian Red Cross.

Her sense that women should be prepared – though for what, it was not clear – had been an emerging concern of many Edwardians. In the years before World War I there had been a growth in organisations across the country where women could learn first aid and simple nursing. The Order of St John and the Red Cross set up a network of local branches, and from these the Voluntary Aid Detachments (VAD) evolved, working closely with the newly formed Territorial Army from 1909.

Some of the well-heeled young ladies who had joined the FANY had access to papa's Motor Vehicle, and on the outbreak of war their driving skills were offered to the government. Who promptly turned them down. But, as with Mrs Stobart, the rebuff merely strengthened determination, and the Belgian and French armies welcomed their offer. Although they were a tiny organisation ('thirty-five gentlewomen') they were of serious intent by then. Off they went across the Channel, kitted out in rather more elegant khaki than others – and famously topped with huge fur coats like mammoth hamsters. They'd discarded the tropical topee – somehow not quite right for a hospital in wintry northern France or Belgium – and showed a tendency to augment the whole effect with silk scarves and snazzy gauntlets.

Some served with the Red Cross in hospitals, others set up soup kitchens and canteens, but it was as ambulance drivers that they made their name. Initially, they were the butt of those who regarded them and many of the other volunteer outfits heading for Flanders as a bunch of lah-de-dah amateurs, but they gripped the wheels of their unwieldy ambulance vehicles and chugged through mud and shot and shell to gain a reputation as tenacious and dashing – and perfectly willing to perform under fire.

They grew in numbers and spread their wings. One part of the organisation, Unit V, was fully integrated into the Belgian army, carrying on working through ninety-nine air-raids and a sea bombardment. They served in all the Belgian hospitals, and some French. (This unit mounted the Guard of Honour for Edith Cavell, the nurse shot by the Germans in 1915, when her funeral cortege left Brussels.) Their routine was to have one FANY on telephone duty to take calls from incoming ambulances, while another girl stood duty out in the open square, ready to direct the unloading of casualties. It was not unknown for the hospital staff to have taken refuge in the dug-outs, while the FANY staff brought in the wounded and gave first aid as they waited for the medics to return to their posts. Not for nothing had they adopted the motto: I cope.

By the end of the war they were regarded as an elite and had garnered an impressive number of decorations, including the first-ever Military Medal awarded to a woman and numerous awards from the Belgians and French. The four hundred women on active service on the Western Front received altogether ninety-five decorations plus fifteen Mentions in Despatches.

The effect on people at home was more than just the impact of individual acts of heroism. Women weren't supposed to have joined a world where medals were pinned to female chests in recognition of bravery absolutely equal to that of the fighting men, and praise had usually been voiced only for the fortitude of women at home confronting the general enlistment of their men; newspapers were generally full of stirring words to stiffen the sinews of being a housewife at home. The *Lady* magazine asserted: 'Think what this has meant for women, gentle and simple, in loss, sacrifice and work! For them there is none of the wild joy of contest, the glow of "esprit de corps", the enheartening sense of comradeship that sustain the men. Their lot has been to live through lonely months of hard routine, thankfully undertaken to keep at bay the haunting dread for ever at their hearts.' The behaviour of the not so gentle and simple clearly didn't fit the general pattern; however, it was all part and parcel of emerging emancipation, and grist to the mill of those who'd fought so hard before the war in the suffrage movement.

For the advocates of Votes for Women, the suffragists, and

their militant sisters the suffragettes, there had been a sudden reckoning in 1914. The various organisations to which they belonged had divided public opinion bitterly through their passionate and sometimes violent campaign prior to the war. Now, as armies mobilised, there was dispute as to whether women were naturally pacifist, or whether their energies should go into supporting the war effort. The arguments were debated very publicly, but took place against a background of war fervour which took hold across the nation: Baroness Orczy, author of the hugely popular *Scarlet Pimpernel* books, founded an organisation which took up the habit of handing out white feathers to men deemed to be avoiding their patriotic duty. Millicent Garrett Fawcett, President of the National Union of Women's Suffrage Societies, stomped the country and turned up in my home town to ginger up the local suffrage supporters. Sunderland women were exhorted to hold fast to their suffrage ideals: her rallying cry of 'Let us show ourselves worthy of citizenship, whether our claim to it be recognised or not' went down well in a hall filled with solid middle-class housewives and a sprinkling of female academics; however, she urged them to remember that, though war would make women's services more conspicuous and prove them to be 'worthy of citizenship', their work in times of peace was just as valuable – for there was already a nagging fear that women's aspirations would be swept away in the manly world of warmongering. She then outlined some of the National Union's plans, which included clubs for soldiers and their wives, the formation of maternity centres and the training of women for acetylene welding. The latter passed without comment in the local newspaper, which had conditioned itself to a regular bombardment of articles from the very active local suffrage ladies.

However, missing from the speeches and tracts and letters to the press from the women who had endured a decade of violent threats at public rallies, physical attacks during demonstrations and force-feeding in prison, was the claim – or even the suggestion – that women should be in the front line alongside the men.

The battlefield was male, and with the exception of the historic or eccentric individual, that was that.

Fighting, uniforms, ranks, medals, all were seen from a male perspective. The Victoria Cross, for instance, inscribed 'For Valour' at the personal suggestion of Queen Victoria and the highest decoration for bravery in the British armed forces, had never – *has* never – been won by a woman. There was, however, a curious moment in 1859 when the officers of the 104th Bengal Fusiliers stationed in India made a presentation to a Mrs Webber Harris. The wife of their commanding officer, she had nursed the men of the regiment during a terrible cholera outbreak which at one point claimed the lives of twenty-seven men in one night. She was given a 'gold representation' of the VC and commended for her 'indomitable pluck'.

The difference between valour and pluck underlined contemporary attitudes. The notion of bearing arms appears not to have been taken up in any serious way by any of the suffrage groups; instead, they took official indifference on any aspect of women's efforts for granted, and set to work immediately to plan, organise and execute a vast range of support activities. They were well versed in getting on with things while being ignored. Alongside their efforts, a myriad of individuals and societies threw themselves wholeheartedly into the huge void in society that quickly appeared as hundreds of thousands of men volunteered for military service. However, their contribution was entirely voluntary – for throughout the war, the government refrained from conscripting women.

When, initially, zealous female patriots proffered white feathers in public to those men they believed were avoiding military service, they were doing so in the knowledge that *they* did not have to head for the misery of the trenches:

> *Oh we don't want to lose you,*
> *But we think you ought to go,*
> *For your King and your country,*
> *Both need you so.*

The music hall stages throughout the land rang to these refrains – utterly un-ironic, utterly sincere, and female voices rang the loudest, with no suggestion whatsoever that women should ever fight alongside their men.

As a small child, I climbed the gilded staircase to the grand vestibule of the Sunderland Empire Theatre. Ancient posters and slightly faded photographs jostled between the dusty red velvet drapes. Women with rather odd teeth and a cottage-loaf of hair simpered next to men in starched collars with boot-polish hair. The great stars of the music hall thought Sunderland a worthwhile detour: the stage was huge and the audiences a challenge.

Away from the metropolitan buzz, with its fashionable society and politically activist suffragettes, Sunderland was a typical northern fastness of heavy industry and no-nonsense Methodism. It was relatively prosperous at the turn of the century, notwithstanding the precarious nature of shipbuilding, with men laid off when a new vessel was named and went down the ways into the River Wear. There were also mining, seafaring and glassmaking, and a rugged work ethic amidst the industrial murk (described in Victorian times with the words 'dirt is the distinctive feature; earth, air and water are alike black and filthy'.) But out of the dirt came rows of substantial 'Sunderland cottages' built for the skilled shipyard workers; many of them were owner-occupiers, a rarity for working people in those days. The town also had slums, clustered especially near the riverbanks, distinguished by stinking middens and communal wash-houses which resounded to the pounding of poss-sticks in the tubs every Monday. There was little available work attached to the yards for women. Some worked in the pottery kilns, and some down at the fish quay. But most worked at keeping home and hearth together, a full-time occupation of scrubbing, cooking, possing and pregnancy.

If you could scrape together a few pence there might be a trip to the cinema – just before World War I there were at least half a dozen, including Hamilton's Flickerless Pictures, but they weren't considered particularly 'respectable', especially for ladies. (The middle classes were only drawn to them when patriotic 'Official War Pictures' were introduced, such as *the Battle of the Ancre*, advertised in the *Sunderland Daily Echo* in January 1917 as: 'The first presentation in Sunderland of this noble and wonderful record of the great autumn battle and the historic introduction of the tanks . . . specially selected popular and patriotic music by our renowned orchestra'. There was also the Bioscope, installed on the stage of the opulent Sunderland Empire Theatre, showing 'Britain Prepared' in 1916, 'a stupendous kinematograph review of His Majesty's naval and military forces'.)

But in an age before radio and television, just twopence could bring you to the music hall and into the presence of glamorous international stardom – in the flesh, on the Empire's stage – as long as you didn't suffer from vertigo, squashed high up in the gallery tucked under the ornate ceiling. If you were flush with money fourpence would get you a little more room in the balcony below, where you could peer down on the nobs in the Grand Tier, who'd paid two shillings and sixpence. Vesta Tilley, along with Marie Lloyd and Hetty King, was one of that small group of women able to throw off the constraints of respectable woman-hood via the stage. In 1907 she topped the bill at the opening of the Sunderland Empire, having just returned from one of her many successful American tours. Tilley was billed as 'London's idol and ideal male impersonator' and one of her most popular acts was Tommy Atkins. At other times she was scarlet-coated, or wore khaki with a Sam Browne belt: the very idea of a woman in a soldier's uniform belonged solely and rather outrageously on the music hall stage. Audiences not only loved her songs, but gawped at the audacity of her appearing in gentlemen's outfits. The very idea of a woman in trousers! Even lady cyclists and horsewomen had the decency to wear long divided skirts. But Tilley's daring was appreciated and her performance was described by the *Sunderland Daily Echo* as 'exquisitely artistic'. (Such praise was not to be sneered at, for in 1908 Charlie Chaplin got not a mention in its columns when he appeared with Fred

Karno's comedy troupe.) Five years later, Marie Lloyd faced the Empire's audiences and encountered their growing reputation as a tough bunch of punters. The greatest of all music hall stars, she apparently found them rather 'difficult'.

In 1914, Marie Lloyd and Vesta Tilley represented exceptions to a woman's lot in life: they earned large sums of money, led independent lives, made indirect references in public to sex, and wore unusual clothes, at least on stage. They were the nearest that working people came to unconventional women. And though in no way 'role models', they wielded influence. In wartime, along with the hundreds of artistes who toured the nation's theatres, they belted out the patriotic songs with both fervour and pathos, and brought home popular sentiment about the war which never failed to stir those in their Sunday-best shawls and straw hats up in the gallery:

> . . . on Saturday I'm willing, if you'll only take the shilling,
> To make a man of any one of you.

In Sunderland, eighteen thousand men took the King's Shilling and enlisted; by 1919, a third had been killed or wounded. Over half a century later, I still heard elderly people talk of Tilley and Lloyd – 'Them canny women in their trews, gorrup like an army lad' who seemed the glamorous, public-spirited glow-worms in the dark of the war.

CHAPTER FIVE

YOUR COUNTRY NEEDS YOU

AVING EXHORTED THE men to go off to war, what should the women do next? With no encouragement from the authorities, but fired with patriotism, hundreds of thousands of women – especially leisured middle- and upper-class ladies – saw some kind of opportunity to enlarge their horizons.

On the home front life began to look like a march-past of alphabet games, with W for Women everywhere: WAF, WEC, WEL, WFL, WFC, WTS, WVR, WL, WFGU. . . Educated women were experts at voluntary work and charitable organisation. Many had no other outlet for their talents and energy. Marriage, with only a few exceptions, put an end to professional work: husbands felt shamed by a 'working wife', and they were supported by employers who dismissed women when they married.

But in 1914, with more women – admittedly small numbers

and among the better off – learning to drive, taking up sport, dancing the Tango and the Turkey Trot and getting a whiff of politics, it was clear to the activists that knitting socks was not enough. Another popular song at the time described 'Sister Susie sewing shirts for soldiers' – surely Susie needed to join the WAF, the Women's Auxiliary Force? Dressed in a blue jacket and skirt with khaki facings, Sister Susie could be gainfully employed as a part-time seamstress, diversifying into first aid, cooking and canteen management, hospital visiting, stewarding in air-raid shelters and growing vegetables for hospital kitchens – and be addressed as Sergeant Susie. Without any prompting, uniforms proliferated, along with quasi-military ranks and structures. It was unconsciously recognised that uniform has its own power, commands respect and endows the wearer with a status – even for the newly employed conductress on the Clapham omnibus or the volunteer turnip-hoer in a Norfolk field.

The field was led by the Women's Emergency Corps, a novel combination of militant suffragettes, feminists and establishment dowagers. And drawing on the previous decade's experience in the suffrage movement, there was a strong feeling that, while the traditional voluntary help of women in time of crisis should be made available, there was also an argument for women who went to work being paid; though often it remained just that – an argument. The Corps quickly diversified into the Women's Volunteer Reserve and the Women's Legion, and khaki became the smart colour to be seen in, although newspaper cartoonists had a field day initially, especially as the WVR had taken to saluting their officers. Hysterical, thought the press. The jackets had a military look about them, all pockets and buttons, and the skirt length was just a smidgeon variable. It seems to have been a personal choice: older ladies didn't show ankles, but the younger spirits flashed their black stockings above their laced boots or sensible shoes; some wore puttees. And all wore hats, dimpled pudding basins with brims – so now I know where our school hats originated.

The aim of the WVR was 'to provide a trained and efficient body of women whose services could be offered to the country at any time' – a wide brief, and one which could be used to assist women whose lives were being affected by absent husbands and loss of income. Dame Helen Gwynne-Vaughan recalled:

> The members wore khaki, did a good deal of drill and were sometimes exaggeratedly military in their bearing, but they did much useful work in canteens and elsewhere, often undertaking scrubbing and other unattractive jobs in their scanty leisure from paid work. Most of them were wage earners who gave their services on night shifts or from six to eight in the morning before hurrying to their offices and workshops. They may be regarded as having made the first reconnaissance in the direction of work for the Army outside hospitals.

And they were followed by the Legion, founded by Lady Londonderry, who gained access to military cookhouses, again extending the army's recognition of jobs which women could usefully do in the services. The Legion both cooked for the army and catered for the mass movement of troops, and also for the increase in wartime industrial employment.

It took only a short time for the editors of women's journals to realise that advice on suitable dress for new surroundings should be offered, backed up by advertisements such as this from the *Lady*:

> 'War work' is rather vague. If you propose to help in a canteen, you will find a trimly-cut coat-overall the most practical, worn over a short skirt and shirt. Certainly pockets are an advantage, almost an essential, and you will find that they are a feature of the strong brown twill skirts which munition-makers and women gardeners are wearing. Beal's specialises in a splendid earth-brown cotton twill skirt of this sort – only 8s 9d; write to Regent Street for patterns.

More adventurously, there were despatch riders – a small number of women familiar with motor-cycles, who confidently acquired breeches and high boots and gauntlets. There was no doubt that a uniform presented women in a public role 'ever so respectably' – even if they were paying for it out of their own purse. However, expensive tailored outfits costing perhaps £2 each – two weeks' pay for a Lancashire textile worker – left many unable to afford to join.

Specialised groups spotted their own niche in the paid volunteer market: the Women's Emergency League spawned the Lady Instructors' Signals Company, which attached itself to the British army in Aldershot, and eventually the School of Women Signallers put out advertisements for 'giving classes in semaphore flags, morse flags, flashlight, buzzer, telegraph sounder etc.'. (No one should sneer at the ladies with their semaphore flags, for I last saw the military using them as two huge American warships steamed past each other in the Adriatic during the Kosovo conflict in the late nineties. The captain of the ammunition supply ship remarked that it was 'a kinda neat sort of communication, no noise, no fuss, and no chance of the enemy listening in'.)

Letters between two of the signalling officers convey the rather odd relationship which these quasi-military World War I outfits generated, as Mrs Brunskill Reid (lieutenant) engaged in a dispute with Mrs Agnes del Riego (her commandant) over a small disciplinary matter: the commandant's letter claims the wartime high ground:

> Now, it must be distinctly understood that I have neither *time* nor inclination to worry over any petty nonsense at the moment. This is War time. There are important matters which demand *immediate* attention and it can but be obvious to anyone that these must come first. Let us rise above all narrow-mindedness because our Country demands of us bigger things, and, in so doing, prove that women can be large-minded enough to work in accord and harmony for a great Cause.

> We meet again at 2 p.m. on Monday to plan out this work. Unless I have all along been mistaken in you (when you realise what is wanted) – you will be at your post, putting Country first. Believe me, my only desire, dear Lieutenant, is to be at one with my Officers, as are my Organising Secretaries and myself.

Rather endearingly, the commandant scrawled under her signature that the letter had been written in 'frantic haste'.

Away from the delights of morse and buzzers, there were horses to be seen to in the army camps: these were the responsibility of the Women's Forage Corps. At its peak it had eight thousand women baling hay, driving horsed transport, chaffing, mending tarpaulin sheets and making sacks. Forage rated as a serious national resource; when a shortage occurred in May 1917 rationing was introduced, and announced in severe terms in the press. The *Sunderland Daily Echo*, for instance, reported: 'The rationing regarding horses is to start at once. No-one will be allowed to feed a horse on oats or grain without a licence, and the Food controller is engaged upon drawing up a scale of rations. Nothing will be allowed for pleasure horses.'

In these circumstances, and after widespread thefts, the Volunteer Reserve provided forage guards for the dumps scattered around the country, and Miss C.F. Shave received her orders from the Forage Committee in Whitehall:

> The Colonel asks me to tell you that you will be required to leave for Ringwood on Tuesday next. . . . Your uniform will be supplied to you at Ringwood. You must provide yourself with a mackintosh, not a raincoat, but a coat that is absolutely waterproof. If you do not already possess one the Colonel would prefer you to obtain an Oilskin from Messrs. Moss. Bros., King Street, Covent Garden. I can give you an order whereby you will obtain it at a cheaper rate. You should also supply yourself with a Fork, Knife and Spoon, or as many of each as you like.
> The Colonel asks me to tell you to be sure and take all the warm

underclothes that you can, a warm woolly scarf, and if you have such a thing, a rug or thick blankets. If you have a dog you may take it with you (not Toy dogs).
  Yours faithfully,
  D.A.F. Codd, Captain & Adjutant.

Captain Codd's attention to detail suggested he knew something about fashion – not for raincoats, but for toy dogs: an impeccably bred pooch had for some time been the indispensable accessory, with *Vogue* magazine stating: 'The Pekingese now Claims to be the Smartest Dog in Dogdom'. Highly recommended were the Boston bull, the Maltese terrier, the Yorkshire terrier, the French bull terrier ('the height of fashion a few seasons ago') and the English spaniel ('in dainty sizes which fit snugly under the arm'). Captain Codd clearly viewed snug-fitting spaniels as highly inappropriate for guarding forage.

Down at Ringwood they perhaps could have done with a nice large Alsatian, as the commander of the guard there, Doris Odburn, remembered: 'The dump was completely open so that anyone could have access to it. It was therefore somewhat farcical that every week I received a top secret envelope from the War Office with a pass word for the day, which I only communicated to the sergeant and guards actually on duty. They were armed with truncheons and whistles but I doubt if they would have been at all effective against an attempt at theft or sabotage.'

Less popular was the call to work on the land: farm work was not a rural idyll of gentle haymaking and picturesque ploughing with placid Clydesdale horses. It was a poorly paid slog with antiquated equipment, which had lowly status compared to factory work, and few women were involved. The Women's Farm and Garden Union existed to look after their interests, and as the war progressed, increased food production brought yet another organisation into being to coax up the numbers willing to speed the plough. The Women's National Land Service Corps was 'a mobile force of educated women to help in recruiting and organising the local labour of women', who would soon discover – dressed in hat, green tie and brown smock – the joys of flax-pulling, egg-collecting and udder-squeezing.

South of London, a motley bunch of girls enrolled in the Women's Defence Relief Corps and found themselves 'harvesting, hoeing, binding and shocking'. Oh, how they took to it, one of them wrote in the *Lady* in 1915:

Many of us were Cockneys who didn't know wheat from barley, And we were all sorts – housemaids, schoolmistresses, singers, painters, writers, women of leisure, factory packers, sick nurses and shop assistants.

It is a healthy occupation. Singers talked of their delicate throats, painters showed their fine hands, ordinary women spoke of nerves and muscular weaknesses. They all admitted in the end that their health and physique were greatly benefited, that the experience had proved invigorating, that they no longer had any nerves.

The pay is not good. A well paid labourer makes £1 a week, and we have to make sure of that. Women working on the land must remember that they have to be careful not to lower the wages for the men who have gone to fight. They must insist on that £1 a week.

With regard to clothes, we found the most convenient garb was shirt, knickers, gaiters, stout boots, shady linen hat, and a long, loose white calico painter's coat; this served instead of a skirt, and came to the knees. – It can be bought for 2s 6d.

Girls got wet through, more than once a day, and needed a change of underwear, and two, possibly three pairs of boots and gaiters (the latter being leather, they were difficult to dry, and remained wet for days).

If they did not have the stoutest possible gloves (housemaids) their hands were cut and torn. They needed several pairs.

The amazing thing about the whole business was the adaptability of women. Who would have imagined that these

delicately-nurtured, highly-educated women would have undertaken the work of farm labourers – and done it?

Proper pay – that wonderful one pound per week – and an outdoor
life: the Women's Land Army and the Women's Forestry Corps
were next in the recruitment drive in 1917. However, even in their
smocks, corduroy breeches and high lace-up boots they were
often regarded as little more than second-best as they harnessed
ploughing teams, wrestled with Heath Robinson harvesting
contraptions and chopped down swathes of English woodland
for ammunition boxes and duckboards in the trenches.

Everywhere, there were exhortations to encourage women to
consider donning gaiters and smocks. Lord Selbourne made a speech
in which he declared: 'Women must take the place of men upon the
land, so that the men can be spared to fight', and newspapers backed
him with descriptions of women ploughing and scattering manure
and asseverations that 'the reluctant farmer is looking about him to
make sure of the necessary labour'. Really? Most farmers actually
thought male pensioners more suitable, leading, reported the
Sunderland Daily Echo, to a sharp set of exchanges among the
members of the Durham County War Agricultural Committee:

> The Chairman remarked that there was what he thought an
> unreasonable prejudice against the employment of women. A
> considerable number were being trained in the County and there
> was a great deal of holding back on the part of the farmers.
>
> Mr Spraggon said some were worth 2s 6d – and others were
> worth considerably less.
>
> The Chairman replied that if they set a low standard of wages,
> they got a low class of labour. A sum of 1s 6d or 1s 9d a day
> was a miserable pittance for more or less experienced women
> workers, who had to walk in some cases 4 miles to their work
> – and pay for their own food.
>
> Mr Spraggon said he was paying by the hour . . . and some
> women were receiving 2d or 3d an hour.

The Chairman thought 2d or 3d an hour was a miserable pittance.

Mr Spraggon replied that if they kept watch upon the women, they would see many of them settling [sitting down] behind the hedge.

The Chairman said he was not surprised. The wages were not sufficient to keep body and soul together.

The pay for the male farm workers was between 6s and 7s a day – some four times what the chairman had described as a 'miserable pittance'. No wonder there was a certain amount of 'settling behind the hedge'. Along with gripes about pay, there were frequent observations on 'the deadly dullness of village life'. To counter this, upbeat articles appeared in the newspapers to convince women that Land Army work had its advantages: 'The long-standing prejudice against farming work for women, as work essentially rough, vulgar and coarsening, is breaking down. This is in no doubt partly due to the fact that large numbers of girls of education and standing have taken up work on the land during the duration of the war.' The implication was that nice young women should not be snobbish about getting their hands muddied. For the reality was that enthusiasm for agricultural work was mainly confined to such middle-class women, most of whom hadn't a clue about the rigours of back-breaking slog in the fields. Their poorer sisters had a better grasp of the toil they'd encounter and they resolutely avoided the Land Army. So the appeals were directed towards the sensibilities of the more refined: 'A woman engaged in ordinary field-work and dressed in ordinary women's garb is not a sight to attract the fastidious; but that objection again is being removed, and it is to be hoped that the fashion set by the National Service girl will be followed by all women workers on the land. The uniform worn by the girls is not only practical but eminently attractive, and no girl need feel her vanity hurt when she sees herself in it.'

These comments came from the Sunderland Women's Suffrage Society, who, although they added the complaint that the 'wages were insufficient', were regularly at pains to stress the 'attractive – and becoming' appearance of uniforms. And if getting prodigiously muddy in a remote field was just too much for the more genteel to contemplate, the *Lady* magazine weighed in with its own suggestions as to how the more delicate might help:

The cry of 'Back to the Land' has been answered by thousands of women, who are only too glad to be able to do really valuable work for their country, but many, though willing, know that their physical health is not equal to work on farms.

Grape-thinning as an occupation for patriotic women is exactly suited to them. It helps to provide a necessary delicacy for our wounded soldiers, and it calls for qualities, such as ready judgement and deftness of hand, with which women are specially endowed. One of the biggest grape-growing districts in England is on the south coast round about Worthing, and in the numerous glasshouses there, since the beginning of the war, hundreds of women have been employed as grape-thinners with great satisfaction to their employers.

Naturally, women dress according to the nature of their work. Caps are 'de rigueur', because the hair must not touch the grapes, and fancy can devise any number of pretty cotton costumes.

Such delicacy was not the usual view of work on the land: magazines joyfully ridiculed the meeting of town lass and country lad, with the popular image of a snooty Land Girl confronting a man busy milking and asking: 'Why are you not at the Front?' To which he replies: 'Because the milk's at the back, ma'am.'

CHAPTER SIX

A FOREIGN CALL
TO ARMS

W HILE THE VOLUNTARY, the part-time and the auxiliary were the norm for much of the war in Britain,
newspapers discovered the excitement of women at
front lines elsewhere. Ten years earlier, intrepid travellers such as
Edith Durham had encountered in the rural Balkans the tradition of 'Albanian Virgins' – women whose families lacked a son,
or who refused to marry the man chosen for them. In return for
forswearing sexual relations, they gained considerable independ-
ence in what was then still a near-medieval society. These women
wore men's clothes and carried rifles like every other Albanian
male. For British readers, eastern Europe was expected to be full
of interesting customs.

A mixture of breathless wonderment, much allied to the word
'plucky', infused the wartime reports from Russia, Ukraine and

Poland. There were instances in the military of 'personation' – with females only discovered when compelled to undergo medical examination. Reports of 'hundreds' of women concealed in the Russian army hinted at a rather exotic and raffish fighting force, but one which was distant in custom and attitudes and would have little relevance to the British Tommy. Certainly there were individuals who distinguished themselves, particularly in the Cossack regiments, but initially many of the tales had the ring of heroic romance. Undoubtedly, the horrendous conditions which nurses found themselves in as they accompanied fighting units led to a number becoming involved in actual combat; however, it was the Russian Women's Death Battalion which eventually delivered to British readers well-documented evidence of women in the front line. Katherine Hodges – later an ambulance driver in France – was in Petrograd (St Petersburg) at the Anglo-Russian Hospital when she was asked to inspect the Death Battalion based in the city.

Every sort and class of woman seemed to be represented. They had not sufficient military uniforms, but they were all in breeches or trousers of sorts, some of them clad in the most amazing hotch-potch of garments. They were young and old, peasant and aristocrat, a most extraordinary mixture.

After the inspection we had an interview with the woman commanding. She asked us if we would stay and join the Battalion to organise a motor-unit for it. We told her we would let her know the next day. After thinking it over very carefully we decided that as she had no cars as yet, merely a vague promise for the future, and as we should have to teach the women how to drive and such mechanical knowledge as we possessed, all in Russian, we thought it was no use attempting it.

The Woman Commandant told us she did not expect women to be any real use as active combatants, but that her whole idea was to restore the morale of the ordinary troops by the force of example. This, I fear, did not work out according to plan for I was told, possibly untruly, I don't know, that when the Battalion left Petrograd for the Front there was a dreadful scene at the station, several of the women being badly man-handled, some deaths occurring as a result. I also heard that every woman carried cyanide potassium, to take if she was made prisoner & feared rape or torture.

Mrs Pankhurst was another observer who passed through Petrograd, drumming up support for the Allies with the same zeal she had brought to the suffragette movement; she too – 'a famous Englishwoman' – was saluted by the Battalion.

A few months later, the reservations voiced by Katherine Hodges were confirmed by another English nurse, Florence Farmborough. Having been a governess in Moscow when war broke out, Florence spent three and a half extraordinary years as a Red Cross nurse serving with the Russian army. She had a keen eye and remarkable mastery of the military realities around her, and also spoke excellent Russian. In the summer of 1917, while with the Russian 8th Army in Romania, she too heard that a women's battalion had been formed – news that thrilled her and the other nursing sisters, though Florence remarked that a woman soldier 'was no unusual sight in the Russian Army'. Two weeks later her admiration was dimmed when news came from the Austrian Front that things had gone badly, and three women were brought in wounded:

The size of the Battalion had considerably decreased since the first weeks of recruitment, when some 2,000 women and girls had rallied to the call of their Leader. Many of them, painted and powdered, had joined the Battalion as an exciting and romantic adventure; she loudly condemned their behaviour and demanded iron discipline. Gradually the patriotic enthusiasm had spent itself; the 2,000 slowly dwindled to 250. In honour to those women volunteers, it was recorded that they *did* go into the attack; they *did* go 'over the top'. But not all of them. Some remained in the trenches, fainting and hysterical; others ran or crawled back to the rear. Bachkarova retreated with her decimated battalion; she was wrathful, heartbroken, but she had learnt a great truth: women were quite unfit to be soldiers.

Maria Bachkarova – or Botchkareva – had led a turbulent life, and had had two violent husbands before she joined the Tsar's Imperial Army in 1914. She seems to have been accepted without undue objections, with her shorn hair and regulation boots, trousers and blouse, and after initial harassment and ridicule was seen as 'a comrade, not a woman'. Her battalion, formed in 1917, attracted worldwide attention and brought forth comment, praise, analysis, shock and disapproval. Nevertheless, its main purpose was not to show that women could fight. Morale was breaking down in the Russian army, and there was disarray after the fall of the Tsar. She argued that 'What was important was to shame men and that a few women at one place could serve as an example to the entire front . . . the purpose of the plan would be to shame the men in the trenches by having the women go over the top first.' A third of them were killed or wounded and many showed great bravery, but they failed to goad the entire front line into action. And when the Bolsheviks came to power some months later, the women were told to go home 'and put on female attire'.

However, worldwide, the battalion's poor military showing seemed secondary in its impact to the very fact of its going into battle, and a world at war chewed over the social and sexual implications of women willing to bear arms. And at least Bachkareva came from exotic Siberia; Flora Sandes, on the other hand, came from Poppleton in Yorkshire.

I first heard of her when I was in Serbia in the early nineties, wedged under a table in a Croat village for several hours while under tank fire. Our Serb interpreter, crammed into a kitchen cupboard under the sink, passed the time between explosions pouring scorn on anyone being capable of heroic feats of valour other than the glorious warriors of the Serb nation. This involved embarrassing questions such as: 'What do you English know about our heroes?' A long silence followed while a tank shell whirred overhead and I searched my memory to locate the pantheon of Balkan warriors on the tip of every British schoolchild's tongue . . .

'Erm . . .'

Another shell found its mark and we all shrieked. A minute later, while bits of suburban villa crackled with licking flames a hundred yards away, Balkan history was back on the agenda. 'What about Vlora Sandees?'

'I'm afraid we didn't do much about Yugoslavia, sorry Serbia, in history,' I replied.

'Sandees was English.'

'Really?'

A tank squealed as it wheeled down a side street and we all cursed the lack of a cellar in the house in which we'd sought refuge.

'Sandees won the Karageorge Medal,' continued our interpreter. 'She fight for Serbia in First World War – you English are all like her?'

Several shells and much mayhem followed, so I was saved from parading my ignorance.

Flora Sandes began conventionally enough – though she had always said her prayers as a child with the fervent request that she should wake the next morning as a boy. She was the ninth and youngest child of a vicar who was originally from Ireland, and she'd had some nursing experience with the FANY and St John Ambulance. Travel delighted her, and she'd once taken a trip – by bicycle – through Central America to visit one of her brothers who was engaged in the building of the Panama Canal. His wife had died, and Flora undertook to bring her very young nephew home, which she did, young Dick spending the first part of the journey through the jungle in her bicycle basket.

Like so many others, at the outbreak of war in 1914 she offered her services, brandishing her first aid certificates. 'I'll go anywhere and do anything,' she said. And like so many others, she was ignored by officialdom. The Red Cross asked if she could join an ambulance unit heading for Serbia. She was thirty-eight and wasn't exactly sure where Serbia was, but left immediately, her baggage including hot water bottles, insect powder and a violin. In her own words she 'was not a trained nurse, but had been for three years an active member of the St John's Ambulance Brigade, so had some idea of the rudiments of first-aid'. Nursing, she thought, was 'surely the most womanly occupation on earth'. Later, she said she had not a thought in her head about becoming a soldier.

Eighteen months later she was carrying a rifle in the Serbian 1st Army, the only British woman officially enrolled as a soldier in World War I. Her transformation, she thought, was not particularly dramatic: 'I seem to have just naturally drifted, by successive stages, from a nurse into a soldier. . . . When the Brigade holding Baboona Pass began slowly to retreat towards Albania, where there were no roads, and we could take no ambulances to carry the sick, I took the red cross off my arm and said, very well, I would join the 2nd Infantry Regiment as a private.' To her Serb colleagues, she was well qualified to serve: she could ride and shoot and drive, spoke French, German and passable Serbo-Croat – and she was English (though speaking with an Irish accent), symbolising a hoped-for promise of support from the Allies, later backed up by her extremely successful fund-raising trips back home.

She had found a true vocation in the army; passionate about the cause of the Serbs, educated and intelligent enough to understand the anomalies of her position and to rationalise it, she fought fearlessly, shot men in combat, was wounded several times, and rose through the ranks to become a sergeant-major and later a captain. As in Russia, there were a number of peasant girls in the Serbian army, including a woman sergeant in Sandes' own regiment. However, the complexities of her position – whether she had become an 'honorary man' and if she needed to prove her claim to serve next to men by being stronger, more enduring and keener to fight than other women, and perhaps some of the men – were the talk of both the Serb army messes and the drawing rooms full of London ladies who'd heard her talk of her experiences. She slept alongside her unit, and was adept at dealing with the sexual approaches and innuendo that inevitably arose. Her method was to cut a figure as a proper serving soldier, trusted by her comrades in arms, and therefore accepted as a person worthy of respect. Rather than being seen as a woman doubtful about her own sexuality or orientation, she mainly had to contend with suggestions that she was just another version of the traditional camp follower, a trollop in uniform. And once a soldier, she reacted with great irritation to the suggestion that she should revert to being a nurse – saying that as a soldier she behaved as one, caring for the wounded only 'between shots', and that as regards the wounded 'we have Red Cross men for first aid'.

Her memories are remarkably matter-of-fact and unromantic, though they ring with the realities of grubby warfare:

> So brutal does one unconsciously become, that when we used to creep out at night on a bombing raid, we always congratulated ourselves on being the most successful when the crash of our bomb was followed only by a few groans and then silence. Were there a tremendous hullabaloo, we used to say that in all probability it meant only a few scratches, or the top of someone's finger – a very sensitive place – taken off.

She endured the hardships of the ordinary soldier and indeed seems to have relished them, carrying her carbine, revolver, water bottle and cartridge belt, and dressing in regulation tunic and helmet. 'We all wear those iron helmets; I hate mine when it is very hot, but love it when we get shelled, which happens pretty often, with very slight cover, and stones and shrapnel come pattering down on it; I only wish on those occasions it was big enough to crawl right under like a snail's shell.' However, her bravery was unquestionable, and she continued to serve even after she was seriously wounded by a bomb on the battlefield in 1916.

> I dare say you've heard that I got knocked out by a Bulgar hand-bomb, so I never got into Monastir after all; but I've had a very good run for my money all the same, as I had three months' incessant fighting without a scratch ... The Serbs are fine comrades. We thought once we should all get taken, but they wouldn't leave me! I've had ever so many cards from them asking when I'm coming back, but as I have twenty-four wounds and a broken arm the doctors seem to think I'll have to wait a bit.

While recovering from her injuries she was awarded the Order of Karageorge, receiving the medal while still in bed; and she did go back, remaining on active service in the Serbian army until 1922. Confounding much of the gossip, she married a Russian émigré officer, but for the seven years during which she was enlisted she was always to be seen in breeches and military tunic, with high-laced boots and army cap.

Living in Belgrade at the start of World War II, at the age of sixty-four she was called up and went off in a lorry with other reservists, even though she had severe disabilities as the result of her earlier wounds. Captured by the Germans, she was taken to a military prison hospital. When a friend visited her and gave her women's clothes, she quickly changed from her uniform and walked straight out of jail, gaining several weeks' freedom until she was rearrested. Her reputation in Serbia was immense, even among the Germans. When they occupied Belgrade, she and her husband Yurie were interned for a short time and she was ordered to report to the local Gestapo. The door was quietly closed behind her and a bottle of schnapps produced, before a taxi was summoned to conduct her home. In 1944, as Russian troops and Yugoslav partisans were poised to liberate the city, the German official made his usual routine visit. Clicking his heels, he said stiffly: 'I will see you next month, madam,' to which she replied: 'No, I'm sorry, you will be leaving – I shall be staying.'

Her family never commented that her military service seemed in any way 'odd', and she herself would talk freely of her time under arms, her sword and medals to hand. She remembered being very conscious of the change to her persona brought about by the clothes, from nurse in skirts to soldier in uniform, writing: 'It's a hard world where half the people say you should not dress as a man and the other half want to punish you for dressing as a woman.'

Those who knew her well later in life, such as Dana Stankovic, describe her as 'a very strong lady, terribly good fun, and a very womanly woman, her hair white from the first bout of typhoid in Serbia'. Looking back on her life, having lived in Belgrade until the end of World War II and then retired to Suffolk, she could recall the frustrations she recorded on returning to civilian life: 'I cannot attempt to describe what it now felt like, trying to get accustomed to a woman's life and a woman's clothes again; and also to ordinary society after having lived entirely with men for so many years. Turning from a woman to a private soldier was nothing compared with turning back from soldier to ordinary woman.'

CHAPTER SEVEN

WAY BEHIND THE FRONT LINE AT HOME

WORLD WAR I saw an intense variety of views set out about the role of women: while Flora Sandes was proving that practical difficulties could be overcome, others were busy touting the strength of women in their domestic stronghold, sending their men to war with uncomplaining determination:

There is only one temperature for the women of the British race, and that is white heat. . . . We gentle-nurtured, timid sex did not want the war. It is no pleasure to us to have our homes made desolate and the apple of our eye taken away. We would sooner our loving, positive, rollicking boy stayed at school. We would much prefer to have gone on in our light-hearted way with our amusements and our hobbies. But the bugle call came, and we have hung up the tennis racquet, we've fetched our laddie from school, we've put his cap away, and we have glanced lovingly over his last report which said 'Excellent' – we've wrapped them all in a Union Jack and locked them up, to be taken out only after the war to be looked at. . . . We are proud of our men, and they in turn have to be proud of us. If the men fail, Tommy Atkins, the women won't.

> *Tommy Atkins to the front,*
> *He has gone to bear the brunt.*
> *Shall 'stay-at-homes' do naught but snivel and but sigh?*
> *No, while your eyes are filling*
> *We are and doing, willing*
> *To face the music with you – or to die!*

Women are created for the purpose of giving life, and men to take it. Now we are giving it in a double sense.

Seventy-five thousand copies of the pamphlet from which this is taken, entitled 'A Little Mother', were sold in less than a week in 1916.

However, it wasn't such sentiment that finally prompted the government to take the giant step and open up the services to women; the appalling casualty lists told their own tale, and more men were needed at the front. In February 1917 the *Sunderland Daily Echo* ran a headline: 'Women as Substitutes'. The article beneath stated that 'Lt General Sir Neville Macready, the Adjutant-General, has devised a scheme whereby women will be substituted for men wherever possible in the Army, both in France and in England, and to release to the Army numbers of men now employed in clerical and other departments.'

Within weeks, the Women's Army Auxiliary Corps was marching and drilling, as thousands of women responded to the posters for 'cooks, clerks, waitresses, driver-mechanics, and all kinds of domestic workers'. At no point was there the slightest question that the Corps was anything but a support unit; the notion of fighting, of being on the front line in some kind of combat role, never arose. It was not part of the debate about what women could contribute to the war; Russian and Serbian women may have been carrying rifles, but such behaviour was foreign in all its meanings to those involved in the formation of the WAAC – and those being recruited. Emmeline Pankhurst, a veteran of suffragette violence, was advocating that women be employed so that 'clerks and cashiers and men behind the counters' be freed up to become soldiers. Despite her fervency ('Sex has nothing to do with patriotism or with the spirit of service'), she did not advocate that women should take up arms. So the call to the services promoted traditional help, in the form of cooking and cleaning and clerking, with the promise of some technical skills training. There was also the lure of 'good wages, quarters, rations, and uniform'.

Whether the uniform was alluring is open to question; a number of the new recruits, like Miss L. Saunders, a teacher, were unimpressed:

> I was sent to Hastings where women were being issued with the uniform of a coat-frock, army shoes and a hat etc – We disliked them all but realised we now had to obey orders.
>
> The coat-frocks were fawn or khaki-coloured with brown collar and cuffs and much longer than we had been used to wearing – we disliked them on sight – and the hats too, but now we knew were an 'Army' and not an individual. The thick shoes too were clumsy-looking and much thicker than what we had been used to. However, we were keen to help win the war, so we dressed as ordered and realised our feminine ideas on dress were now of no account.

The uniform had had the benefit of some female thoughts from the most senior women brought in to organise the women's services, Mrs Mona Chalmers Watson and Mrs (later Dame) Helen

Gwynne-Vaughan: 'Unwisely', said Dame Helen later, 'we thought that breast-pockets would emphasise the female form and decided against them; ... The skirts were full and considered most daringly short, as they were twelve inches off the ground. At first we had little, tight-fitting khaki caps with khaki crepe de chine veils at the back. Later, they were replaced by round, brown felt hats – known to their detractors as "baby boys" from their resemblance to the hats worn by children.' But there were problems, according to Dame Helen: '... the women provided their own underclothes, and, while these were often excellent and usually neat and appropriate, instances occurred when they were in rags or hardly existed at all.' She had encountered the common fact that many women from poor backgrounds wore the very minimum of underclothes – knickers were an upmarket item.

Overall, the idea was that the women should look as military as possible – but the War Department was very wary of giving them traditional ranks and badges. Fleur-de-lis and roses with crossed stalks were deemed suitable, rather than the usual crowns and laurel leaves. 'Regrettable,' was Dame Helen's view of the titles given to officers: 'officials'; 'other ranks' women soldiers were to be 'members' while NCOs became 'forewomen and assistant forewomen'. In France a need arose for some term for the rank and file, the 'private', and Dame Helen recalled: '"Worker" was decided upon at a conference at GHQ, the suggestion that "amazon" was appropriate being mercifully disregarded', and she added, 'I suspect these titles were given "to keep us in our place".'

And all these women were legally civilians: what had been formed were the Women's Services, and women were not being integrated into the armed forces. Besides, the War Office determinedly referred to them as 'camp-followers'.

Quite a number of the women who joined up had had other wartime jobs, often in factories, and the chance to join 'the army' offered a glamour that had hitherto been lacking; whether they had their dreams fulfilled is doubtful. Olive Taylor, after domestic and munitions work in Lincolnshire, volunteered the moment she saw a poster and was sent to Aldershot:

> When first called on parade while still in civvies, one of our number – a very prim lady – turned up with an open umbrella. She said she had never gone out in the rain without an umbrella. The barracks were very spartan and food poor and there was very little of it.
>
> A sergeant of the Coldstream Guards was awarded the doubtful honour of teaching us to march. I don't suppose he really wanted that position, but he really inspired us with his 'Put some swank into it, girls' and soon he had us smart as a regiment of guards and was quite proud of us. We would do a seven-mile route march during the morning and be given two halves of a potato and a little gravy for lunch, along with a little boiled rice and two stewed prunes, and then be on another long route march, before bulling shoes, buttons, badges and chin-strap ready for the next day.

The pay, for women who'd been lucky to earn £1 a week – or even less – in domestic service seemed reasonable, but it was hardly riches: even the junior officers were only on just over £2 a week. Olive earned a mere 10s, out of which came laundry, breakages, and 'all our underclothes, including even corsets, by hook or by crook – three sets of everything ... so we could never have a treat'.

However, the mere fact of belonging to something officially recognised as of national importance, and being paid by the government, was a novelty to thousands of women. Hitherto women had usually only been recognised through their family ties, existing as someone's daughter, wife or widow; they still had no vote and they had little connection to officialdom. As for appearing in public in uniform, the sight of lines of women in khaki caused no little amazement. Corrall Smith, an enthusiastic girl who thought her own uniform 'topping material – and looks jolly when worn properly', observed some of her friends drilling in Hyde Park watched by 'two very grandes-dames who were looking on with puzzled faces. After a few moments, one put up her lorgnette and turning to her companion said "What on earth do those creatures in khaki think they are doing?", and her friend replied "Don't know I'm sure, but they are something connected with the Salvation Army" – however this is exceptional and mostly the public are awfully decent and kind.'

Olive Taylor discovered a different attitude during a rare outing from another camp, near Woolwich:

> Some of us looked forward to going into Woolwich and perhaps enjoying egg and chips, but we were subject to such insults in Woolwich that we never tried again. Here we learned for the first time that we were regarded as scum and that we had been enlisted for the sexual satisfaction of soldiers. This, after the way we had worked ever so hard, and put up with so much deprivation for our country's sake, was absolutely terrible. We were broken hearted about it and never went into town again. What a treat it would have been to be able to enjoy egg and chips, something some of us had never even tasted.

To add insult to injury, in the military camp there was rigid discipline which prevented casual socialising by Olive and her friends:

> 'Out of bounds' was three miles away and one was not allowed to speak to a soldier within bounds. This was a very serious offence and repetition of it could get a girl dismissed the service for unsatisfactory conduct. So if a girl became acquainted with a nice soldier she had to run three miles, say 'hello' and run back again. There were some very nice boys among the Irish Guards, but we could never trust a Coldstream Guard. They would even threaten to throw us into the Brookwood Canal if they couldn't have their way with us and they seemed to have only one thought in mind. What did it matter to them

if a girl lost her character and ended up in the workhouse with a baby?

Moral panic seized the authorities regularly when considering the impact of women in the army. As hundreds were sent across the Channel to work in offices and canteens in France the generals worked themselves into a tizzy, observed by the redoubtable Dame Helen Gwynne-Vaughan, newly appointed Chief Controller overseas.

> I soon discovered that the objection to the employment of women was almost universal. The Services, of all professions, had naturally the least experience of working with women . . . then there was the question of the relationship between the women and the soldiers. At an early conference at GHQ it was agreed that they were bound to make friends and to walk out together. It was better that they should do so openly with the full approval of the authorities than surreptitiously as an exciting adventure. Nevertheless, a general officer protested that 'if these women are coming, we shall have to wire (off) all the woods on the Lines of Communication'. That was more than I could stand, and I answered: 'If you do, sir, you will have a number of enterprising couples climbing over.' The woods remained unwired.

Notwithstanding the fact that the women were putting up with poor rations and very basic accommodation – lack of beds and surfeit of rats seem to have been a common complaint – and working long hours, the general public back home was very open to the suggestion that northern France was heaving with sexual liaisons. *The Times* carried an article casting aspersions, and it reached Aileen Woodroffe at her VAD (Voluntary Aid Detachment) post in No. 30 General Hospital in France:

> I travelled on a tram today with some of the WAAC. They do not do well running about on the loose, not speaking the language, being rather conspicuous and exceedingly stupid and giggly . . .

The article in *The Times* describing a WAACs camp is really here – quite close; they really are a quaint lot of females, but a tremendous boon and joy to the men stationed about here. It is really rather amusing to see the couples 'roamin' in the gloamin', after 6 o'clock, and having ham and eggs together, what the natives think of the proceedings, I can't imagine, but the fact that it is a recognised thing to have a WAAC friend is no doubt quite helpful, as there really is nothing for these wretched men to do after hours.

After some months, the *Daily Sketch* tried to calm matters down with a measured article: 'One hears wild and varying stories about the relations between the rank and file of the WAACs and regular army. Joining the WAAC isn't like taking the veil or starting on a career of unbounded sky-larking. Army men and Army girls meet on ordinary ground and are friends in a normal above-board fashion as girls and men are friends in civil life.' Perfectly reasonable, but certainly not the stuff that was doing the rounds as common gossip: the whole enterprise was rumoured to be a disaster, with hundreds of women said to have been sent home to give birth to illegitimate babies. The best bit of scuttlebutt was a widely believed story that a soldier had to be posted as a guard outside 'the WAAC Maternity Home'.

Dame Helen tackled head-on the problem of men and women alongside in war, and saw it primarily as something which bothered the public more than the serving personnel. Pregnancies were dealt with in a low-key manner, and sympathetically, with the women being discharged on compassionate grounds; this was despite the background in 1917–18 about which she said that 'the occurrence of pregnancy was a reliable criterion of the "moral" position' – in other words, there was no getting away from the public's judgement that pregnancy indicated how women were conducting themselves, regardless of the circumstances. She saw the association between the women and the troops as 'inevitable' and endeavoured to make it 'ordinary, friendly, fraternal' rather than something that happened by stealth, 'an exciting adventure, stimulating passion':

> No doubt the association of war and love is one of the oldest in our make-up and goes back to the roots of the subconscious and the earliest combats of two males for the female. Possibly the unconscious desire to leave offspring when life is to be risked is also a factor. At any rate, it is clear that, in war, the man is more ardent, the woman more vulnerable. Administrators had to be warned to keep a vigilant and kindly eye on these possibilities. It was not, as might at first have been imagined, the pretty and attractive girl who needed their special care. She was accustomed to admirers and already knew the technique. But the older, plainer woman might find it intoxicating to be the cause of competition, and gratitude for this fillip to her self-respect might be her undoing.

Despite the sensible and level-headed approach of Dame Helen, there was still much gossip back in Britain: and she was none too impressed when a committee of five ladies selected by the Ministry of Labour arrived in France to investigate 'immorality'. After much nosing around, they were reduced to producing a report which revealed that the WAAC were 'a healthy, cheerful, self-respecting body of hard-working women, conscious of their position as links in the great chain of the nation's purpose, and zealous in its service'. Anyway, Dame Helen had been brandishing statistics: under three per thousand single women had become pregnant since joining the army. It was a figure considerably lower than in civilian life back home.

Pregnant or not, the women were not intended to be in the front line. However, by 1918 there were frequent air-raids well behind the lines, raising for the first time the spectre of women – other than medical personnel – becoming battlefield casualties. Dame Helen recorded in her diary:

On the night of 21st–22nd May, Camp II, Abbeville, on the Montreuil road, was hit by the largest bomb that had been used up to that time. So extensive was the crater that the Commander-in-Chief himself came to see it. The huts were blown to pieces, only the mess hut and cookhouse being left. Uniforms were scattered far and wide, some garments landing on the branches of the trees. The women themselves were in open trenches and were none the worse. I was able to be at the camp early and was proud to find that, in spite of their disturbed night, every woman, – how clothed I will not attempt to say – was in her office or cookhouse at the normal time. From that incident arose a tradition of the Corps that, whatever happened, Queen Mary's Army Auxiliary Corps [recently renamed thus – a much-desired seal of royal approval] reported punctually for duty. During the day the area controller issued fresh clothing.

Eight days later an aerial torpedo exploded in a trench, killing eight QMAACs outright; one died later of wounds and six others were injured. There was a funeral with full military honours the next day, aeroplanes flew overhead, and a large number of soldiers and several officers fell in behind the members of the Corps who followed the gun-carriages. Dame Helen found the press waiting back at HQ 'all wanting a story and prepared to execrate the enemy for killing women': She continued, 'Up to this time the only women of the Army killed in theatres of war had been hospital personnel under the Geneva Convention. It was an entirely new idea that since we were replacing combatants, the enemy was entirely in order in killing us if he could.' However, she had no desire for headlines which concentrated on gender, and impressed on the journalists that in the circumstances the enemy could be excused.

Back in Aldershot, twenty-year-old Olive Castle was busy being a military waitress:

Mountains of washing-up, and cleaning after every meal,

windows and muddy floors to be scrubbed, 500 pairs of army boots in all kinds of weather, every day, four times a day – you can imagine the state the floor was always in. We had no kneeling mats of course (not in the Army!) so we did it all on our hands and knees. We took turns in doing that job, and that was what I was doing at 11.05 am on Nov 11th, 1918, my overall filthy with mud from the scrubbing, when the official wire came through and the Colonel summoned all the cadets on to the parade ground in front of the mess-room for a very important announcement. He quietly told them the news of the signing of the Armistice at 11 o'clock ... We all tried to 'do our bit' to help in the time of our country's need. Nothing spectacular, perhaps, just jobs which needed to be done at the time.

If the WAACs were well distanced from the traditional image of soldiering, then the women who joined the WRNS were equally far from the life of a sailor. Any girl with traditional aspirations of gadding about piratically on the high seas in war would have got as far as Lowestoft in 1918. Clerks, canteen assistants, storewomen and messengers – no wonder the WRNS eventually acquired the unofficial motto 'Never at Sea'. Ports and harbours were the only water they saw, and there was no intention ever to have them near ships, never mind on them. Superstition, prejudice, and lots of argument about 'skirts and ladders' kept the Wrens ashore.

The Admiralty, immensely amnesiac on the subject of women aboard ship in the preceding centuries, had not even tolerated female civil servants on the outbreak of war. Vera Laughton Mathews, who later commanded the WRNS in World War II, was testily informed in 1914, 'We don't want any petticoats here.' They finally caved in three years later and advertised for 'Women in the Navy ... the members of this service will wear a distinctive uniform, and the service will be confined to women employed on definite duties directly connected with the Royal Navy.'

Admittedly they were a fully-fledged service, and led by women, and the first senior administrators had had the good sense to argue against the title Women's Auxiliary Naval Corps. However, a large number of them had the rather odd designation of 'Immobiles', meaning that they served in their own home towns; the 'Mobiles' joined the Senior Service not to see the world, but merely to see another part of the British coast, or possibly a 'balloon station'. Here they wore navy blue, their skirts several inches nearer the ground than those of their army colleagues. A sailor's blue and white collar was eventually added because the girls disliked their plain collars, and would insist on borrowing from their navy boyfriends. One small group was trained as wireless telegraphists at the signal school at the Crystal Palace, known as HMS *Victory VI*, where in January 1918 Vera Laughton Mathews, then a young officer, presented herself to the commanding officer. She described him later as having a 'really progressive mind', and, indeed, he was preoccupied with matters which seventy years later the services in the Gulf War had still not resolved, remarking: 'Well, Miss Laughton, you and I are both in the same service and there are certain things which have to be discussed. Now regarding the matter of lavatories . . .'

Just occasionally some of the WRNS worked aboard ships in harbour, their soufflé-like caps emblazoned 'WRNS' rather than the sailors' 'HMS'. But most were as nautical as a fishwife as regards life on the ocean wave. On the other hand, their officers did pull off one small coup, acquiring rather amazing large tricorne hats to go with their well-tailored suits. Not that this was entirely accidental: there was already a certain distinction between the services, and women who went into the WRNS were regarded as a cut above the WAAC. Class differences, after several years of war, were as distinct as ever, and army recruitment had drawn heavily on working-class women. On the other hand, the WRNS often came from families with a long naval tradition, and soon found themselves wrestling with rules which forbade them from socialising across the ranks with the Royal Navy – whose officers were their brothers, fathers and cousins. Dame Katherine

Furse, their first Director, who had years of administrative experience as co-commandant of the Voluntary Aid Detachment, soon sorted out these awkward social hiccups, though she had a keen sense of the need for propriety among her 'gels', recalling with a certain satisfaction in her memoirs that her girls were sometimes referred to as the 'Perfect Ladies' – and also the 'Prigs and Prudes'.

If life on the ocean wave was just a dream for the WRNS, so was the notion of being a magnificent woman in her flying machine. But life in the Women's Royal Air Force at least permitted women to enter the world of 'string-bags', 'pups' and 'moths'. Flying had already garnered its own aura of romance – dashing pilots in fragile biplanes, the freedom and progressiveness of those who were 'air-minded'. When the RAF and the WRAF were created simultaneously, in April 1918, there was a spirit of cooperation in that women were welcomed who, in addition to the usual clerical and storekeeping tasks, would take an interest in what went on behind the propeller.

When she was about eighty, Mrs P.L. Stephens from Yorkshire recalled her days as one of the first members of the WRAF: 'How good it was to be young at that time,' she said, and remembered leaving munitions work in Lincoln for 'something more exciting':

Looking one day at the notices at the local Labour Exchange, I saw a most unusual one: 'Wanted, female motor-cyclist, for RAF Scampton Aerodrome – apply within'. I promptly did so and the man said 'I'll 'phone the Drome now, so wait'. Quite soon, a Sergeant arrived on a motor cycle with sidecar, and after looking me over said 'Hop in – I'll take you up to the Camp and give you a try-out'. I said 'No, *you* hop in the sidecar, and I'll drive you to Scampton'. So, I was signed on, and found myself the only girl amongst some few hundred men – attached to the Transport Section. There were five other motorcyclists, and they did not give me a warm reception – thought I'd be a nuisance, I suppose, and they did *not* speak to me at all for some considerable time. All I said to them was 'Just leave my machine 3764 *alone* and don't take it when your own is out of order – because mine *won't* be!'

. . . No uniform at that stage was provided, so I had to buy some khaki breeches and shirts which I tried to conceal under a rather old and grubby rain-coat! I loved my job – worked hard and was very happy – taking officers to the Station, collecting them from there, delivering goods to Married Quarters, taking the Pay Sergeant to collect cash from the Bank for the men – On Sundays I had to collect the Padre from a near-by village, for Church Parade. I think he was always rather nervous whilst in my care as he usually found other Transport to take him home afterwards.

Sometimes my task was grim – to take the M.O. to a crash within reach of the Aerodrome. Once nothing left save the young Pilot's cap badge – he was very young and a great favourite – I remember the Adjutant broke down and wept when the M.O. told him there was nothing to be done – Scampton was a RAF Training Station and there were many casualties . . .

Once I had to go before the CO on a 'charge'. The charge? Pilots had followed me in their planes, flying very low over the hedges bordering the road on which I was going on duty (no-one in the side-car) into Lincoln, and they waved to me – and I – of course! – waved back. This behaviour had resulted in a cow being killed that cost £20. What had I to say? Nothing. I was a docked a day's pay, and the CO before discharging me remarked 'No further proceedings, on the understanding that you wave to me when next I salute you from my plane.'

A good number of women who joined the WRAF had already served in the WAAC or WRNS and they transferred to the new service. Somehow, the British class system wormed its way into the image of the new services – the WRAF women were considered 'nice', just as the Wrens were 'perfect ladies'; the WAACs, on the other hand, were just 'women'. The nice air force girls got a new uniform, which took an age to be distributed. It finally turned out to be very like the WAACs', but grey-blue. However, at least a tradition had begun of women being involved with actual aircraft, for many worked on the machines, and some were offered flying instruction, giving a boost to what was already significant participation by women in aviation, and eventually leading to some of the first women in the services taking up combat operations towards the end of the twentieth century.

By the end of World War I over a hundred thousand women had been enrolled in these auxiliary bodies, and a vastly greater number had put on the uniforms of the various voluntary organisations. In nearly all instances they had managed their administration themselves, without resorting to having male superiors. They had had a very public role, their dress marking them out as taking part in national affairs, and some had been paid by the state – a novelty at the time. They'd made a significant contribution to breaking the image of frail, dependent women who were frightened by the drums of war.

CHAPTER EIGHT

MUD AND BLOOD

ICTORIAN PRUDERY AND snootiness about nursing had ebbed away as the twentieth century began. Caring for the sick and wounded in war had become acceptable again, with the added imprimatur of the great Nightingale. The FANY and Mrs Stobart's nurses had beaten almost everyone across the Channel on the outbreak of World War I, though there was little appreciation of the horrors they'd face. However, more than an inkling of this soon turned up on the home front.

In my own town of Sunderland 400 miles north of the trenches in Flanders, it arrived by train only weeks after the declaration of hostilities. On to the platforms came the cot cases and the sitting cases – wounded men who were just a fraction of the massive disbursement of casualties nationwide. The first party of one hundred men went to the Royal Infirmary and were immediately subjected to the ministrations of girls from my old school, who were already knitting socks and making shirts for the Durham

Light Infantry. 'Some comforts and luxuries not provided by the hospital regime' were delivered. Senior girls were sent to help in the Red Cross Auxiliary Hospitals and crosses of flowers were taken to the graves of two Canadians and an Australian who died in the Infirmary.

The girls of the Church Schools Company embodied the determination and patriotism that flamed up in 1914, exhorted by their redoubtable headmistress, Miss Ethel M. Ironside, late of Cheltenham Ladies' College. Three months into the war she wrote that the girls were to pray that God would defend the right, and that when peace came the school would have nothing to look back upon of which it need be ashamed . . . and to keep perfectly serene and full of hope. Women at home, she continued, must make the men in the services feel that they realised 'the glorious stock from which they are sprung, a breed which through all the ages had stood for valour and for courage that laughs at difficulties'. Later, for good measure, she named the school houses after Royal Navy ships – HMS *Tiger*, *Panther*, *Swift* and *Drake*.

None of this was in any way exceptional; Sunderland was typical of the phenomenal reaction to the advent of war. The huge response to the need for men to be nursed and cared for was manifested immediately, and ranged from teenagers doing needlework at War Hospital Supply Depots in County Durham to the departure of the first QAs for France a mere fortnight after the declaration of war.

The first ship which crossed the Channel in the vanguard of the British Expeditionary Force also carried Maud McCarthy, matron-in-chief to the British armies in France. Australian-born, she'd already served in South Africa during the Boer War, and ahead of her were five years running a nursing operation that extended south to the Mediterranean, sustaining a reputation that 'defeat was unknown to her'.

But at a time when few women, with the exception of the moneyed upper class, travelled abroad, most of those QA sisters who crammed into the first troop trains would not have had the slightest idea where they would eventually serve. World War I saw hospitals and casualty clearing stations in Egypt and Gaza and Jerusalem; in Basra and Baghdad in Iraq (then Mesopotamia); all through Serbia and Macedonia and in Sofia, Bulgaria. In Dar-es-Salaam – capital of the former German East Africa – with mosquito boots, veils, thick puttees and quinine essential, and in Tbilisi in the Caucasus. And on the hospital ship *Kalyan* anchored in sub-Arctic waters off Archangel, with sheepskin coats, serge gloves and fur ear-muffs very necessary. The scale of operations was astounding, as were the challenges confronting women brought up in late Victorian and Edwardian society. Sybil Harry wrote from the Salles Militaires Hospice Unité:

Saumur 22/10/14

It would amuse you to see some of the improvised utensils in the wards – I don't think the hospital has more than 5 small basins for the 200 wounded! As to a bucket it is unheard of, and we use anything from teapots to dustbins. Hot water is as scarce as whisky, and one only gets about 1 pint daily, so the cleaning has to be done cold. There is no installed hot water system or lights of any sort. The water is heated on gas rings, and the wards by tiny oil lamps I am sure were used by Henri II who lies buried near here.

When the operations are after dark, it is a perilous proce-dure to get your case down a flight of stairs & thro 3 large wards, with a match. I have sworn at the men until I have got an oil lamp from the office, which is now placed on the stairs. I do so long for some reliable bearers. These are awful, & so rough. When they are tired, they dump the stretcher on the ground, regardless of place, and sit on the side. The orderlies are soldiers too mad or too bad to fight, so their capabilities are what you would expect. They never cease smoking, they shave not, neither do they wash, & their garments are anything to be found. We have just trained one he should not expecto-rate *on the floor*, but I know he does it the minute we leave the ward. All these little things provide amusement but are most irritating at the end of a worrying day, however there is a war on and one must not grumble. Visitors to the Cardiff Hospital cannot get an idea what war is really – if I told you some of the things that come in here, you would be horrified and it's just as well that England has not seen yet these remains of what were bright young men brought in to die in a few dreadful hours.

The military nurses were in the vanguard in the first few weeks; large numbers from the Territorial Reserve followed. So did a number of individuals who were utterly convinced they were going to do good, never mind their lack of qualifications, permission or any knowledge of bed-pans. Most were rather grand and, contrary to the scepticism of the officials, proved themselves to be a very tough bit of the upper crust. Foremost, in all senses of the word, was Millicent, Dowager Duchess of Sutherland and daughter of the 4th Earl of Rosslyn, who spent several weeks intimidating army officers – mainly German – as the British Expeditionary Force ran into serious trouble and trench-lines began to define the battlefield. A former Victorian society beauty, also a published poet and a keen rider to hounds, Millicent was resourceful and flamboyant. She crossed the Channel, clad in elegant cap with the red cross prominent on her cape, and descended on the unsuspecting front lines – only to find herself under bombardment and on the wrong side. Totally unflustered, she marshalled her team of eight nurses and a surgeon, treated wounded French and Belgian soldiers in Namur while the Germans looked on flummoxed, and then got everyone safely back to England by dint of doughty common sense and all the social clout she could muster. The authorities were embarrassed, but their grumbling came to nought as Her Grace raised money, collected her supporters, and headed back to Calais to run one of the best Red Cross hospitals throughout the war. She was only outdone in style by the younger and prettier Duchess of Westminster, who ran a smaller hospital at Le Touquet. Not content with touring the wards with her wolfhound in tow, she and her lady helpers used to greet the wounded on their stretchers having donned tiara and evening dress – the duchess was a firm believer in positive morale-building. (Her hospital made a specific contribution to medical history in the war, for it gave the post of registrar to Charles Myers, a former editor of the *British Journal of Psychology*; he'd been told he was too old to volunteer, so he arrived to be taken on by the duchess. However, as casualties mounted he was commissioned, and took on specialist work in other hospitals where he coined the term 'shell shock'.)

Back in Britain, there was a host of women volunteering; several thousand of them belonged to the Voluntary Aid Detachment, the VADs who'd been trained by the Red Cross and St John Ambulance. In blue dresses – or grey for St John – with a prominent red cross on their starched white aprons, these middle- and upper-class girls who were usually occupied with tea-parties and visiting and were now oh-so-keen to 'do their bit' flocked to local hospitals and embarkation ports; initially, however, both prejudice and the feeling that the war would be brief left the War Office unconcerned about using them.

Just two years earlier there were only 553 qualified women doctors in Britain, and they'd been traditionally corralled into looking after women and children. Medical schools were bastions of prejudice, so it was not surprising that these educated and intelligent women who'd survived pompous surgeons and hostile professors were made of the right stuff when it came to war. They also knew that they'd be wasting their time in taking on the War Office. Dr Louisa Garrett Anderson and Dr Flora Murray went straight to the French Embassy in London, were not properly understood because of their rusty grasp of the language, and breathtakingly contrived to head for the Hôtel Claridge in Paris four weeks later as the Women's Hospital Corps. They were seen off by Louisa's mother, Elizabeth Garrett Anderson, who must have felt such pride to see her daughter as chief surgeon leading a trained team, dressed in green-grey uniforms with matching hat, back to the city where, in 1865, she'd become the first British woman to qualify as a doctor. Had she been twenty years younger, she said, she'd have led them herself.

Up in Edinburgh, Dr Elsie Inglis had offered to supply qualified women doctors and nurses but been turned away by the War Office with the cutting remark: 'My good lady, go home and sit still.' She did no such thing, and started raising funds to set up her own operation, the Scottish Women's Hospitals. A seasoned campaigner, Dr Inglis had been involved in the suffrage movement and was aware of the power of publicity; she'd already established two hospitals in Edinburgh before the war, and was a born organiser. Dr Inglis reckoned that the only way to make proper use of women's skills was to create hospital units staffed entirely by them, giving women the chance of performing surgery – and to offer these units to other governments (the British, even though mid-war they bowed to the inevitable and used women doctors, still withheld officer status and refused to employ them on the front line). She was incredibly successful, and though hers was only one amongst many women-only outfits it was the largest and best known, sending over a thousand women abroad.

At the Abbaye de Royaumont in France, a deserted Gothic fright and home to a lot of bats, her organisation soon set up well-equipped wards, with many of the two hundred beds individually sponsored: my local newspaper, the *Sunderland Daily Echo*, received regular reports on the Abbey, which contained 'a Sunderland bed in the Millicent Fawcett Ward'. Miss Marjorie Starr wrote home to Canada of her life there as a VAD in 1915:

Monday 13th September: Nothing different today. Same old rush, two operations. We had a great old time with one poor man this morning. He has all the tendons and nerves of his arm mixed up, and had them operated on again, so they had to be dressed, and the agony was so terrible they gave him chloroform, and it took 6 of us to hold him, he struggled so when he was going under. I had to hold the arm for the dressing and got well sprinkled with blood and pus, as he was very septic and

Taking over from her father, the official Bill Poster and Town Crier in Thetford, Norfolk, pastes up the call for women in World War I.

Joan of Arc, *painted by Peter Paul Rubens, c. 1620*

Sarah Rosetta Wakeman, alias Private Lyons Wakeman, enlisted in the Union army on 30 August 1862. She told the recruiters she worked as a boatman – which was true – but omitted to mention she was a woman

Kit Ross in the uniform of the Scots Regiment of White Horses